THIS WILL BE MY UNDOING

HARPER  PERENNIAL

NEW YORK • LONDON • TORONTO • SYDNEY • NEW DELHI • AUCKLAN

THIS WILL BE MY UNDOING

LIVING AT THE INTERSECTION OF BLACK, FEMALE, AND FEMINIST IN (WHITE) AMERICA

MORGAN JERKINS

HARPER ⬤ PERENNIAL

HarperCollins books may be purchased for educational, business, or sales promotional use. For information, please email the Special Markets Department at SPsales@harpercollins.com.

FIRST EDITION

Designed by Jamie Lynn Kerner

Title page and chapter opener art ©photolinc / Shutterstock

Library of Congress Cataloging-in-Publication Data has been applied for.

ISBN 978-0-06-266615-4 (pbk.)

18 19 20 21 22 LSC 10 9 8 7 6 5 4 3 2

FOR YOU

Contents

THIS WILL BE MY UNDOING

I am the first and the last
I am the honored one and the scorned one.
I am the whore and the holy one
I am the wife and the virgin
I am the barren one and many are my daughters. . . .

DAUGHTERS OF THE DUST

1

MONKEYS LIKE YOU

WHEN I WAS TEN, THE ONLY THING I WANTED WAS TO BE A white cheerleader. Bone-straight hair. Thin nose. Saccharine voice. Slender body.

When I was ten, I realized that I was black. In some ways, that had nothing to do with actual cheerleading, but rather with what blackness meant, writ large, learned from the experience of trying to force myself into this pristine, white, and coveted space, which spit me out before I could realize how much I had been abused.

I grew up in Atlantic County, New Jersey, just twenty minutes from Atlantic City, depending on how fast you drive down the expressway or Black Horse Pike. There are not many places in Atlantic County you can go where the last name Jerkins is not known—my uncles Rodney and Freddie have achieved incredible success in the music industry, producing hits for artists like Jennifer Lopez and Brandy. Maybe this was why I was generally popular with the black and Latinx students in my school. Teachers asked if my uncles could pop in to the class to supplement their math lessons, and aspiring producers wanted to know how they could get in touch with them. There might have been incidents when I was called ugly, or rejected by some guy whom I basically didn't know but was infatuated with nevertheless, but that was all they were: incidents, moments. They were not experiences that defined my childhood, or me.

As a kid, I loved TV. I religiously watched shows like *Saved by the Bell* and *Lizzie McGuire* and slept through the weekday nights while *The Facts of Life* played in the background. And there she was, always: the cheerleader. She wasn't always blonde, but she was always white, skinny, and desirable. She was equally powerful and pure.

When I was ten, the only thing I wanted to be was a white cheerleader.

CHEERLEADING TRYOUTS FOR ELEMENTARY SCHOOL WERE UN-der way, and I knew that this was my chance. If I made the squad, it would be easier for me to make the team again and again from middle through high school. All prospective squad members were mandated to attend nightly sessions in our elementary school's cafeteria in order to learn a dance routine, gain tips on how to impress the judges with our energy and attitude, and practice our jumps. I was one of only four black girls in a room of about thirty white girls. The others were Tanya, a second-generation Jamaican-American; Ruby, whose name matched her beauty; and an Afro-Latina whose name eludes me now. There were no Asians, no Pacific Islanders, no Native Americans. If you blinked, you might not have noticed us four black girls there. The cafeteria was large, and the whiteness was blinding.

Although I could not stir up the strength to lift my pudgy body (with 34C breasts, to boot) into the air to perfect a pike or tuck, I made up for it with my enthusiasm. I wasn't as popular with my black and brown classmates as I was with the white ones, although I was one of only a few black girls who regularly mingled with them. To this day, I'm not sure if it was due to circumstance or colorism, my light skin often associated with whiteness, my identity regularly mistaken for biracial. Nevertheless, I wanted equal social standing in both spaces. Just to be in the presence of white girls—mainly those who had been cheerleaders for years, those whom all the boys, both white and of color, wanted—I felt privileged. I hoped that if I were adjacent to them, then some of their desirability could lather me like soapsuds to the skin, polishing me off until I was just as white as them. I scrutinized how easy it was for them to make their bodies fly through the air, how graceful their movements were. Every gesture seemed like a dance. I might have noticed these talents when they sat beside me in class or brushed past me in the lunchroom line, but these sessions isolated them so I could study them a little bit more closely. Spatial boundaries did not apply to their bodies. They could move anywhere they pleased. Their bodies knew this even if their prepubescent minds didn't. There was no place that they could not go without being acknowledged: not the playground, not the classroom, not the lunchroom, and most certainly not cheerleading practice. I had only a faint awareness then that being born in white skin, they had been groomed for this kind of dominance.

Unlike the cheerleaders in sitcoms and cartoons, these white girls weren't stuck-up and rude. On the contrary, they were quite helpful, giving me tips on how to smile when I appeared in front of the judges and how to stretch so that I could improve my momentum for the jumps. Were they nice to me because of my uncles, perhaps? Because I was light-skinned? I wasn't entirely sure. I was ten; I didn't know myself. I exhausted so much of my mental energy hoping that a nonblack girl would swallow me into her identity that I never spent much time alone with me and only me. Looking back, they seemed to talk to me more than they did Tanya and Ruby, and both of them were darker than a brown paper bag. But could it have been because I made more of an effort to grovel? All of my closest friends were older girls of color who weren't trying out or interested in cheerleading at all. The more I invested myself into becoming like those white cheerleaders, the less mental space I devoted to my actual friends. If I could not be a white girl, then I could mimic one until anyone who saw me would think that my skin was a costume. I thought myself very ugly. I had ill-fitting glasses, a large overbite, plaited hair that made me look like a kindergartner, and an adult woman's body. I felt caught between two worlds, that of children and that of grown-up folks. I dreamed that cheerleading would provide a middle ground where I could be popular, envied by children and adults alike for my youth, fortitude, and beauty. These white girls were well aware of their beauty and how much power it yielded. They wore their hair in high ponytails that swung whenever they moved. They discussed who had the most tubes of lip gloss, whose butt looked the biggest in Limited Too jeans, who shopped where for bras. There were of course factions, and enemies swung the word "slut" around because there was no worse insult to direct towards another girl. Unlike with white girls, whose repeated mudslinging seemed quite boring and nonchalant, black girls' conflicts were more directed and violent. If you were talking behind someone else's back, that person confronted you. If that person was bigger or more popular than you, you either surrendered through crying (i.e., self-abnegation) or apologizing. But even then, a fight was still a possibility. In our world, the most immediate solution to silencing someone was through physical force. Many black girls, including myself, thought of our strength through physical force as a way of protecting ourselves. White girls weren't expected to be strong; they didn't need to be. They were already supported, cared for, and coddled enough. Fighting, for them, would have been extravagant— what did they have to prove?

THE NIGHT OF TRYOUTS ARRIVED. I HAD BEEN PRACTICING IN my room every night; my mother encouraged me, told me that I "had it in the bag," that they would be a fool not to let me in. When she was a child, she didn't make her cheerleading squad, but then one girl fell ill and she was accepted into the elite. I felt like I was a legacy, that I was destined to follow in her footsteps by becoming a cheerleader and, in the process, I would become beautiful through whiteness. I don't know what fueled my mother's desire to become a cheerleader. I never asked because I was afraid that in turn she would ask me the same.

Families lined the elementary school hallways with beach chairs, blankets, and picnic baskets full of food because they knew that tryouts and decisions would all happen in one night. The judges were the cheerleading coaches, those who also taught us all the vocabulary, jumps, and dance routines. My mother and I held hands to pray that God would hold my fear at bay. I knew the dance steps. I'd practiced them while walking downstairs for breakfast and dinner. I'd practiced them on the way to the bus stop. My smile was congealed on my face; I was excited before my moment began. My confidence was so overwhelming, so filling, that I refused to touch any food or drink before it was my turn.

Every white girl walked out of the cafeteria where the tryouts were held with a smile on her face. She hugged her mother, high-fived her, or simply walked over to her spot by some wall in the hallway to relax until the moment of truth. When my name was called, I walked in with two other white girls and the Afro-Latina. The judges, all white women, smiled and welcomed us. Their hands gripped their pens, ink bleeding onto their evaluation sheets. I don't recall breathing. Once the music began, I danced our routine almost like I was a programmed machine. I just went, my body moving and cutting through the air. I made eye contact to let them know that I was there, and they watched me. When it was time to judge our jumps, the Afro-Latina was the first to go. We were standing on opposite sides of the cafeteria, with the white girls couched in between us. Our order was not intentional, but nevertheless it was significant to me; we stood as poles for the white girls to remain at the center.

The Afro-Latina faltered on her jumps. She forgot what one of them was and stood there with a surly look on her face. She jutted her right hip and began to roll her tongue in her mouth. *Oh no*, I thought. I knew those gestures well. I'd seen them in my mother and aunt when they were fed up. She was returning to being a girl of color. When she forgot her steps, she remembered who she was in that room full of white women. She was paralyzed.

"Do you want to try again?" one judge asked.

"I don't know," she replied. She was not upset. In fact, her expression spoke of exhaustion. There was nothing left for her to do, so she stood there and we moved on.

I knew that I had to be better, not only because I wanted to be a cheerleader, but also to signal to the judges that I wasn't like her. We might both have had light brown skin and the same wooly-textured hair, but we were not the same. As I'd expected, I did my jumps without so much as wobbling when my feet returned to the ground. I walked out of that cafeteria feeling as airy and euphoric as the white girls. I couldn't feel my actual body whatsoever. I imagined, I almost believed, that my body had no restrictions. I was limitless, white.

Hours passed as we waited for the results. We had gotten to the tryouts at around six p.m. and didn't hear anything until about nine, ten o'clock. The cafeteria doors opened again, but this time, the judges were coming out rather than inviting girls in. The entire hallway was silent. I could hear my heartbeat thumping in my ear and an incessant ringing in the other. They called names one by one: white, white, white, white, white, white, white, white, white, white, white, white, white. White girls hugging their white mothers. White girls surprised at the results, covering their mouths and squealing, "Oh my God." White girls surprised, white women judges holding back their excitement for their new, and yet old, team. The one judge speaking stopped, and they returned to the cafeteria.

I blinked and a tear rolled down my cheek. One became several. Several became innumerable. My mother spoke with Tanya's mother and they deliberated going to the administration to "talk about this." I did not know what "this" meant. Ruby, throughout it all, smiled and gathered her things. As for the Afro-Latina, I don't believe she and her family stayed until the end. My mother tried giving me a CD to cheer me up, but I could not help but think that something was terribly wrong, not so much with the judges but with me. Maybe I didn't smile enough. I didn't recall smiling, but that's because I had been trying to focus. Maybe I was too fat. Maybe I wasn't beautiful. That had to be it. Because I was not a cheerleader, I felt like I was sentenced to eternal ugliness.

I got over the results within a few days because I had another kind of drama unraveling in my life. One of my closest neighborhood friends and I were fighting. I do not remember what it was about, but it had to have been something stupid, because what was that serious at ten and eleven years old? The Internet was starting to get popular—more of our fighting happened over AOL instant messaging than in person. We might have typed curse words to each other, talked about each other's hair and clothes, but there was one comment that brought my fingers to a standstill: "Do you know why you didn't make the cheerleading squad, Morgan? It's because they don't accept monkeys like you on the team."

This "friend" was Filipina, and several shades darker than me. I had heard rumors that her family was racist and this was why I was never invited into her house, but I'd never thought she was infected, too. After all, she wore fitted hats, dated black guys, and knew the lyrics to more rap songs than I did. She moved through black spaces with so much fluidity that we accepted her as one of our own. But when she called me a monkey, I thought back to the first of those nightly prep sessions. There was no amount of practice or smiling that could obscure the inescapable problem of me being a black girl. Did those white girls look at me as a monkey who had to be treated with artificial cordiality so that I wouldn't act wild or aggressive? Did I transform into the character of a monkey when I performed in front of those white women, subtly begging for their acceptance without questioning it? Suddenly, I understood more about race than I ever had. It didn't matter if my "friend" was wrong. I didn't make the team, and therefore, she knew that I was inferior. Unlike her, who ingratiated herself with black people and moved into our spaces, I could not perform well enough for white girls to claim me as their own. It wasn't simply because I wasn't good enough to make the team. I couldn't make the team because I was not human. And when I looked at myself in the mirror, when I kissed my mother good night, this feeling of being the monkey, nonhuman, haunted me. I should've known my place. I should've known that when I was around my black friends, I was who I was, and when I was in a white space, I wasn't afforded humanity. And maybe that was what I was really trying out for, not a cheerleading squad, a chance to be a person. Did I smile to be less threatening? Did I dance to prove that if I kept moving, I could avoid being confined by their preconceived notions of who I was? Just what exactly needed validation?

WHEN I WAS THIRTEEN YEARS OLD, MY MOTHER'S BOYFRIEND, a revered and well-liked Rowan University professor and psychologist who we liked to call "Z" for short, rose from our leather sofa and bent down on one knee in front of her. I heard my mother's surprised scream of delight and that was it because I was already on my way back upstairs to hide. I'm still not proud of what I did. She had survived two previous marriages, one marred by physical and verbal abuse and the other by cheating, and a jilting. She deserved all the love in the world, yet I refused to watch it blossom because I knew that my own life in Atlantic County was about to be over.

Z had tenure, but my mother could conduct her real estate business from anywhere. It was only logical that we move closer to the university. After Z proposed and my mother accepted, my older sister Patricia found me upstairs in the bathroom.

I couldn't look her in the face as I asked her, "Do we have to move?"

"Yeah," she replied weakly. "But it will be okay. You'll be fine."

I wanted to believe her, but this move would not affect her. She was eight years older, had graduated from high school at sixteen and moved out of the house shortly afterwards. As my mother and I packed all of our belongings away in preparation for our move to Williamstown, a suburban neighborhood less than fifteen minutes away from Rowan's campus, I yearned for her companionship.

My mother tried all she could to get me excited about Williamstown. We drove past our new home in a residential lot. It was noticeably bigger than our old one, complete with four bedrooms, a conjoined bathroom to every room, and a large basement. I saw some cute boys hanging around Main Street and that made my heart flicker, but that flame of excitement disappeared as quickly as it came.

Egg Harbor Township, where I had previously lived, and Williamstown had similarities. In the towns themselves, there were the usual bowling alleys and movie theaters. Families resided there for years, and their children almost always came back to perpetuate the cycle. But Egg Harbor Township at least had Atlantic City nearby, and from more rural Williamstown, with its Heritage's Dairy store, acres upon acres of farmland, and common sightings of wild turkeys, you had to go a long way to get to Philadelphia. And Williamstown was far less racially and ethnically diverse than Egg Harbor Township.

I was more warmly received by the boys when I started eighth grade at Williamstown Middle School. Immediately, I latched onto and befriended a Colombian named Caterine— one of only a handful of Latinx in the school—who was in many of my classes and showed me the ropes. As she shuffled me along different hallways, the black boys did double takes, sometimes going as far as impeding our path to introduce themselves to us before saying one last hello when we parted ways. I was the new girl, and in this small town any novelty was exciting. Lunch came around, and I was informed through whispers that I was "fine." The speed at which a teenager's tongue moves could compete with the speed of light.

Caterine didn't ask me about where I'd moved from, how many siblings I had, or what music I liked. Instead, she would pass notes in class, asking me if I had a boyfriend or whether I was a virgin. When we went to gym, she gossiped with the black girls about who slept with whom over the summer and whose pussy smelled like tuna. I was both revolted and intrigued. Who knew that thirteen-year-old girls could talk like such grown women? One time during lunch, I was teased for not knowing what an orgasm was, as though that were something I should've known at that age—like knowing how babies are made. In Williamstown, sex was more palpable, and I could feel its presence like a gnat buzzing near my eardrums. A girl outright told me, "Dick is like food. Once you have it, it's a must," and this was *before* she accused me of wanting the guy who'd taken her virginity the summer before, influencing her friends to ostracize me. But this paled in comparison to the harassment I'd experience from a new student the following year.

Jamirah moved to Williamstown from Virginia the summer before our freshman year of high school, and at first she seemed just as mild-mannered and meek as I was. The most popular girl in our year was Tiana, who was two years older than everyone else, and one of the most unapologetically black girls I'd ever met. During our industrial science class, she would often go to the nearest mirror, take out a toothbrush from her purse, scrape gel onto it, and smooth down her edges. Her laugh could be heard from one end of the room to the other, and she expressed her excitement by clapping her hands. On the flip side, whenever she was disgusted, she pursed her lips, rolled her eyes, and jerked her neck. I was always nice to Tiana because that was my natural disposition and also because I was afraid of her. Everyone was—hence her popularity.

Although Jamirah and I were both soft-spoken, Tiana must have recognized something in Jamirah that she didn't see in me. Maybe it was because Jamirah immediately started following Tiana around, and consequently Tiana swept her up quickly. Soon, Jamirah became just as boisterous and brash as Tiana and her crew. It didn't bother me much in the beginning because I wasn't black like them. They were the kind of "black" that I was not supposed to be, a.k.a. *those* black people, the ghetto ones, the ones who made the rest of "us" look bad. My mother taught me to suppress those habits that Tiana was known for. As opposed to the other black girls, who wore graphic design T-shirts and hip-hugger jeans, my mother dressed me in cardigans, argyle socks, and plaid skirts so that I would "look the part" at all times.

Tiana and most of her group were in remedial and college-prep classes, and I was on the honors and advanced placement track, working in courses where I was one out of only a handful of black kids, and that is a generous estimate. The worst times for me were the periods when I wasn't distanced from those who were not on the same academic trajectories: lunch and gym. I hated these egalitarian periods most because they were when I received the most abuse from Jamirah and, to lesser extents, from her friends.

At lunch, she'd yell at Tiana to draw attention to my neck or lack thereof while I was literally sitting right across from her at the same table. She made fun of my wardrobe, my intelligence, my speech, my looks—any and everything that made me a person: "Look at her. She ain't got no neck. What the fuck you got on? The fuck is that shit?" I was always afraid that at gym, she would push me face-first into one of the lockers and start a fight out of boredom. Both she and Tiana frequently made idle threats about wanting to jump somebody while we changed, our half-naked bodies further emphasizing just how susceptible we all were to an ambush.

It was a kind of meanness that I have never seen matched. I did not know why Jamirah hated me so much. We didn't like the same guys, didn't frequent the same places after school, and didn't speak much to each other. But perhaps this in itself was the reason. I did not want to be boisterous and brash and assert myself in the throes of the black community at high school. I maintained my timidity, preferring to be invisible so that I could commit to my studies and escape from Williamstown in four years. I confided in a few friends about Jamirah's relentless bullying, and they urged me to retaliate, but I was too afraid of the consequences. If I swung on her—even though I'd never fought before—I'd get suspended, and that would mean that I'd get a bad reputation with teachers. I wouldn't get those stellar recommendations I needed for college. I dreamed of getting an MD from Columbia and someday taking over my father's medical practice. I feared I would be categorized as "one of them": those black girls who were on the bad path in life and would end up pregnant before graduating high school, the black girls who would probably go as far as community college before settling for a waitressing job at a nearby Applebee's.

Even in middle school, the black female body was always a target for destruction. Violence was a legitimate way to resolve arguments. Talking was not a conclusion but rather a trigger. You fought someone who talked badly about you or someone who wanted your man. In other words, you fought to maintain your space in an environment where your place was already on the margins. For what black girl wants to be even more invisible than she thinks she already is? Fighting was a way to assert that you were present and in motion. Fighting brought you respect that institutions refused to give you. I thought I wanted to be invisible. I wanted those institutions to respect me, and I believed I could earn it through silence, through assimilation. But my path of nonviolence only led to a cascade of madness.

I didn't need to lie in bed with my curtains closed because

whatever light permeated my windows could do nothing to dilute the darkness welling in my spirit. I spent many nights hidden underneath my covers, hot tears streaming down my puffy cheeks, unable to voice my pain even in private. In my head, I replayed my daily humiliation in front of all my classmates, and there was no sign of it letting up. I thought of no other escape than to commit suicide, but despite having called the local suicide hotline, I had no concrete plans for flinging myself out of this world. I just hoped that I would one day disappear and find myself on a transcendental plane where there was no more pain and humiliation. Secretly, I envisioned that all the tears I cried would drain my body and my mom would eventually find my desiccated corpse in my bed. I prayed to God to take my misery away from me, and my prayers became more impassioned the longer the harassment continued.

After realizing that my despondent behavior was not symptomatic of PMS—since it dragged on for weeks—my mother ultimately found out what ailed me. She spoke to the Williamstown High School administration about my problems and they did nothing, chalking up the bullying as a rite of passage. She then suggested that I transfer to a private school but I was too afraid to start over again. Since I could not be protected by the higher powers, one of my sisters offered to come to the school in sneakers, ready to fight Jamirah. I rejected both suggestions because I wasn't entirely lonely. I had a few friends, one of them a boy named Dennis, who told me that Jamirah's envy was the reason she bullied me. Dennis was one of my closest friends; he had moved to Williamstown the same year as I did. We lived only five minutes from each other and spoke for hours through the telephone on the weekends, talking about anything and watching shows together. He was my saving grace, and I figured it was better to suffer in high school with him by my side than to transfer to another school and start all over again. Not to mention I thought the change in schools, along with classes and extracurriculars, would make it difficult for me to get into a top college.

I had moved to another lunch table to sit with upperclassmen to avoid Jamirah at all costs. One of my friends called me back over, and Jamirah eviscerated me with such panache. She smiled, flicked her hand at me, and asked, "Why you talkin' 'bout me? What's good?" I stuttered through it all, explaining how I had other friends and that she was mean to me, which led me to leave the table. Finally, Jamirah stood up from the table and ended with, "I don't give a fuck about you. So you can kiss my ass," and protruded her ass before sashaying to another side of the room.

The friend who betrayed my trust smiled and sucked her tongue. She said, "You betta' say something back! Don't let her get away with it!" I assumed my friend must've told Jamirah why I moved, for how else could she have known? I left quietly, on the verge of a breakdown. I spent the next period silently crying while taking a test, the social studies teacher hovering over me but never asking if I was okay.

A sick game was played: I was tested on whether I could assert myself. I was not only supposed to "buck up," or be aggressive, but also prepare to fight. Jamirah pushed me to leave that lunch table. She pushed me out of that space. Although I found another one, the underlying point was that I needed to reclaim my original space even if I had no intention to return. Instead, I cried and fled to another table with a shattered sense of self. I hated Jamirah, I hated my friend, and I hated every single black girl who laughed at me that day.

I blamed myself for not saying what I'd really wanted to say to Jamirah. I'd wanted to narrow my eyes at her, smirk, and say, *No, I don't give a fuck about you. I'm prettier than you, I have longer hair than you, I'm smarter than you, and I'm going to be more successful than you. You know it. I know it. Teachers know it, and there is nothing that you can do to change what's already been set up for your life. You'll hit me because you already know you failed and every time you see me, you see the reflection of your failure. That's why you're mad, and frankly, I would be, too, if I were you. But thankfully, I'm not.*

I considered myself to be the bigger person because my passiveness had afforded Jamirah power that she would never have outside of Williamstown High School. I thought that because of the tone of her voice, the profaneness of her mouth, and her lackadaisical attitude towards school, she was going to end up a statistic, whereas I—if I remained respectable with my honors and advanced placement courses, preppy clothes, and clean hair—was set to bypass all of that. But I also regretted not doing more to defend myself. I entertained the thought of calling the police on Jamirah, perhaps even lying and claiming that she had put her hands on me or she was a threat to my safety. The officer would take one look at me and then at her and tackle her. I would watch with glee as her body was pinned to the ground by an officer two to three times her size. It would not have mattered to me that this officer was protecting me not because I was afraid, but rather because, out of the two of us, I was the closest approximation to whiteness and its rules. I wanted her to be humiliated as she had humiliated me, and if I could not do it myself, I would rely on the institutions to do the job for me.

It was a violent anti-black-girl fantasy of which I am, almost a decade later, beyond ashamed. We were two kinds of black girls raging for dominance and assertion. I wanted us to get along, and I thought that such harmony was contingent upon white acceptance. I hated black girls like Jamirah who did not conform to respectability politics; I hated their loud voices, their cadences, how they gelled their baby hairs with toothbrushes, their eye rolls, their neck rolls, the way they clapped their hands in exhortation, their tongue-sucking in disgust. They didn't like me because I did conform. Jamirah relied on that validation from within, and I from without.

A FEW MONTHS LATER, I LOST MY DOONEY & BOURKE WRIST-let, which was a status symbol for white girls back in the mid-aughts, and I panicked. The wristlet contained both my wallet and cell phone, and I was sure that I would never see either one again. I checked in every single one of my classes, spoke to teachers, scanned every hallway, but nothing. When I finally went down to the main office to call my mother to pick me up from school since I had missed the buses, I found my wristlet—with my wallet and cell phone still inside—behind the receptionist's desk. Someone was kind enough to bring it there, and I soon found out that that someone was Jamirah and Tiana. Blindsided is an understatement. I felt as small as the wristlet itself. Why would the two girls who'd made my freshman year a living hell be so kind as to return my valuables? Perhaps because, regardless of what they felt towards me, those valuables were mine. I imagined all the people who might have passed by my belongings, all of those who left them there. But neither Tiana nor Jamirah was going to allow anyone, not even themselves, to take from another black girl. In a strange twist of events, they looked out for me. I thanked them, but I wished that I could've done more.

Not too long afterwards, Jamirah stopped me in the hallway at our freshman semiformal, to tell me how beautiful I looked. I thanked her; there was nothing else to say. By this time, I had found my outlet for my anger: writing. The allure of creating a new world in a better and more peaceful universe, where I could have new friends, was unexpected, and powerful.

Jamirah ended up leaving Williamstown after freshman year. Years later, I found her on Facebook and discovered that she'd moved back to Virginia and had two children. I could still sense her bravado in the way she pursed her lips for mirror selfies, and I smiled. I thought about reaching out to her to say hello, but I never went through with it because I didn't know what to say. Maybe I could ask her for an apology, but then again, perhaps her returning my Dooney & Bourke purse and complimenting me on my looks was exactly that. Maybe I could apologize for looking down on her—I'd never said I did, but I knew she knew. Maybe I could wish her happiness, but I wasn't sure that I wanted that for her either. The pain she inflicted on me hasn't entirely gone away, just as I haven't entirely forgiven myself for what I felt towards Jamirah and her crew. I've never wanted to return to high school, even in my memory. This is the only time I've written about it, and I did so because it felt important—this is what black femaleness is, or at least part of it; this is the violence we hurl at one another.

I didn't want to be friends with Jamirah, and I'm sure she didn't want to be friends with me. I suppose all I wanted to do was remind her that she did not break me. And maybe I would wind up thanking her because if she never teased me, then I would never have discovered my true passion for writing. I would also thank her for teaching me how to assert myself more because years later, once I went to college, I became more assertive. My behavior might not have totally matched Jamirah's, but my passion was just as obvious, if not more so.

I AM TERRIFIED BY THE THOUGHT OF RAISING A BLACK DAUGHTER who will also have to fend for herself. At times, I wonder how I managed to survive. Something happened to the black girl, the young black woman, that I was. I fell into the chasm between what I thought I was, what I wanted to be, and how others saw me. I still have not been able to reconcile these selves with much clarity, and fueled by the vestiges of this trauma, this poisonous place of insecurity and inflated self-importance, I write for that girl, for that young woman; I write for me now; and I write for you. Because a monkey is what I never was, but a black woman is what I had to become.

Growing up as a black woman is different. It prepares

you to remember that you have to navigate two worlds. In our predominantly white world, you will never be white. I'd assumed that playing by its rules would insulate and distance me from other black girls; I'd depended on white supremacist tricks to make me feel as if I was better than them. Although I never confronted Jamirah with these lies, I feel just as reprehensible for housing them in my heart.

As an adult woman, I can feel Jamirah in my voice whenever I get mad. That agile cadence, that unparalleled wit, which renders my profanity as poetic as lines from a Shakespearean sonnet, rhythm and all. I know now where that anger, that primal need to make myself known, comes from. Belonging to the world of black women demands strength, on-your-feet wit, and aggression, because space for and by ourselves is small. You either assert yourself or learn to do so through humiliation, exposing who you really are: just another black girl fighting to exist.

After that lunchtime confrontation with Jamirah, I could never go back to being the black girl I once was. Her words corroded me, and that rust birthed a harder person, one able to see weaknesses in others and strategize about how to keep myself protected by any means necessary. But that corrosion also reminds me to check myself whenever I feel like my lighter skin color, or education, or behavior gives me some kind of inherent superiority over other black women. Basically, I needed her. I believe we needed each other.

This book is the balm to my soul and my gift to you. The desire to be the cheerleader while being seen as the monkey, the strain to be passive over the demand to be aggressive, the bullying, the conflict—all of this takes place on the battleground of being born both black and female. We cannot afford to believe that any part of ourselves gives us an edge over another. Ultimately, we are all fighting. I intend to fight those on the outside rather than those on the inside who are just as victimized as I am. I cannot divorce either part of my identity, and I recognize now, as I excavate my most painful memories, that to try to do so would be to understate their impact on my psychology.

There is equal value in race, gender, and class, for each trait refracts a different light onto another, which is why I write. Someone may have read these two anecdotes from my childhood and believe that this is what happens to *all* little girls. It's true that we are *all* victims within a patriarchal society and we must fight. But the fight to empower all women under the veil of feminism has historically and presently centered white women. The word "all" switches to whiteness as the default—this is also why I write. When black women speak about themselves to those who are not black, somehow our interlocutors get offended that we dare speak about how both race and gender affect us. Somehow, our acknowledgment of our blackness and womanhood causes others' brains to short-circuit because they have never been encouraged to focus on the type of person who has been dehumanized and neglected for centuries. The only way many can make sense of us is by looping us together with white women because their whiteness, their illumination, provides some kind of intellectual relief that erases black women all over again.

And to that I say this one-sided feminism is dead. This book is not *about* all women, but it is meant *for* all women, and men, and those who do not adhere to the gender binary. It is for you. You. Our blackness doesn't distance us from other women; however, it does distinguish us, and this requires further understanding. At the same time, my story is not a one-size-fits-all tale about black womanhood. This book is not your resolution but the continuation of your education, or maybe the beginning. We deserve to be the center; our expansive stories are worthy of being magnified for all their ugliness, beauty, mundaneness, and grandeur. I will not baby you. Instead, I will force you to keep your eyes on me and, in turn, us, and see the seams of everyday life that you have been privileged to ignore but that have wrecked us. Some of us are still wrecked. I am admittedly so in some ways, which you will know about soon enough. But in many other ways, our community has been strengthened and that's why I am here and you are continuing to read my words.

And to that I say, welcome.

Let us begin.

2

HOW TO BE DOCILE

1. When your black girl child exits the womb and you hear her loud wailing, savor and remember it for as long as you can. That's the loudest the world will ever allow her to be in a room where multiple people are present.

2. If she's ugly, hide her face with a lace-trimmed handkerchief and tell passersby that she's sleeping. If she's beautiful, hand her off to strangers so that they can talk about how pretty her skin is or how many curls they can count on top of her small head.

3. When she's approaching six or seven months, where it's time for her to start speaking, teach her "Dada" first so that she knows that whatever comes out of her mouth is a symbol with a point of reference and that

reference always returns to man. Man is the establishment and system, and don't ever let her forget it.

4. When that black girl child can learn to form full sentences, teach her early on never to ask questions, especially if the interlocutor is a man. She must learn submission early if she is to succeed in life. Don't allow her eyebrows to raise when she sees the women in her community laugh and call the boys "fresh" when they question things. Smack her face if you must. An emotionally inexpressive black girl child is one who keeps herself alive.

5. If she relaxes her posture and her legs begin to spread, hit both kneecaps with an open palm or the back of a pan so that she associates opening herself up with pain.

6. If she spends too much time running after the boys or allowing them to chase after her, call her a fast-tailed girl even if she won't know what that means. Remember: she's not allowed to ask questions. And frankly, she's better off that way. Ambiguity will undo her sooner rather than later.

7. When she bleeds for the first time, tell her how inherently dirty she is and that what she is down there is nothing but a cesspool of stench and waste rather than a channel that brings forth life and takes in pleasure. Tell her that she's a woman even if she has no hair besides that on her scalp and arms or no sprouting breasts because the weight of that word "woman" makes her feel as if she can tip the scales. It's not about what she feels but what she is made to think that will do her in.

8. You can pinpoint the exact moment when she begins harboring sexual feelings for the opposite sex: her stare lingers a little longer than normal; her voice tapers off while she shakes her head and tucks her bottom lip into her mouth; her blushing, her lack of eye contact. Tell her what happens to black girls who want to be "fast." Tell her that they will get pregnant and never achieve anything. Tell her that the boy will leave her and that he won't give her the respect of his pants hitting the floor when it's time to do what grown folks do. Tell her, tell her, tell her. And before you know it, the next time she so much as lays eyes on another man, her vaginal muscles will tighten. Her opening will produce an extra layer of skin as a fortress so that no man can get in, and if he does, that in and of itself is her punishment for not keeping it tight.

9. Instruct her that being complimented on her looks is much better than being complimented on her brains. Everyone wants a black woman who makes him or her feel at ease. Her face is the easiest way to comfort people, and if she isn't pretty, then her silence is even more necessary, for it is better to be present in the room than never in it to begin with, and she must get in, even if she cannot participate. She must access whatever it is that they have by any means necessary.

10. If she tells you that a man calls her pretty, pour yourself a glass of Merlot because men don't give compliments easily, and then figure out a way to get her vaginal muscles to unwind themselves. The only thing worse than being a black woman is being a sin-

gle black woman, and it's time to reel a man in. Black is ideal, but whoever will have her works, especially if she's doing well professionally. Ain't too much of her kind up at the top, and love is love anyway. The only thing worse than a successful black woman is a single and successful black woman.

11. Tell her to let the man be the man. Don't argue with him. Don't share an opinion unless he asks her to. Let him be right even when he's wrong. If she takes care of him in this way, he will take care of her.

12. Tell her that when he's ready to make love, she should lie on her back and spread her legs as far as they can go. She'll remember you beating her knee-caps with open palms and backs of pans, but at least this will distract him, breaking through her skin to find a home inside of her. If she screams out in pain or cries, he'll probably ask her if she wants him to stop, although this is not what he actually wants. Urge her to not make him stop or slow down. Instead, tell her to focus her attention someplace else, even if that place is unreal. Let her think of Elysian fields where black girls receive more mercy. She can stay there until he comes. Then after that, she should either rub his chest, watch him as he rests, or bring him some food from the kitchen, before he wants to do it all over again.

13. Once he decides that she doesn't excite him anymore but is too comfortable to officially break up with her, he'll cheat on her and you must blame it all on her. There must've been something that she was doing

wrong to not keep him around, and she better make things right so that she won't embarrass you.

14. If they do decide to get back together, she'll shrink even further. The next time you see her, you'll mistake her for your own shadow for her light will be gone.

15. When she finally enters those prized spaces that you told her about as a child, she'll have everything she'll need to succeed: looks, deference to man, suppressed sexuality, silence. A good ol' twenty-first-century mammy, ready to give, ready to serve. She will be the talk of the town, the new Negro socialite, the one whom countless black girls must emulate if they want to get anywhere *and* have a man on their arm while doing it.

16. After a few years, you will notice some other things about her: she's getting physically smaller until she needs a booster seat to sit at the table. Her man can't enjoy fucking her because he feels like a pedophile, but he feels too comfortable to leave her so he cheats on her again and with more than one woman this time around.

17. Her voice gets higher- and higher-pitched until the register she reaches is so high that no human ear can detect what she's saying, not even her own.

18. Without her body ever reaching orgasm, without ever housing a penis that recognized that her vagina was not a ground for domination, the only hole that hasn't closed up down there is the one through which she urinates. Neglect will do that to the body.

19. Soon, she won't be able to move. Doctors cannot diagnose her as comatose simply because she can't speak when spoken to. They believe she can still feel; she simply cannot move. Perfect, you think. The less she moves, the more mobile she can be. People will remember just how comfortable she made them feel, and they will take pity on her.

20. But they don't. Her name rings a bell, they snap their fingers to try to conjure the letters of her name, but they ultimately give up and return to eating their watercress sandwiches or cheese and charcuterie. They do not remember her name or how she made them feel. They blame it on her not speaking up enough when she was around. Her body collects dust. She stops menstruating. She stops urinating. She does not speak. She cannot eat. You are waiting for her to die, but not sorrowfully because this was the plan all along. Black girl children aren't supposed to live; they're supposed to exist. When she dies, you know you should not mourn for her because now that she's dead, she lives more expansively than ever before. Where there is no man, there is no world that can make her feel less-than. Yet you do mourn for her because maybe it was not her time to go. Maybe there was something else that you could've done to make her shrink but not die, as if one can happen without the other.

21. Nevertheless, you fold back into the community, where you teach other black girls the same ritual but with more fine-tuning. You're sure that you'll get it right this time. The world forgets the former black girl child when they accept another token who whets their palate like a new flavor of the month. The man finds another woman, and he makes love to her with all his clothes off, pants and boxers hitting the ground, watch on the nightstand, and that woman comes over and over again. When he closes his eyes the moment after orgasming, he sees your child's face and silently thanks her for preparing him to be the man that he is today.

22. This is how a black girl becomes docile.

3

THE STRANGER AT THE CARNIVAL

I LOVED AMUSEMENT PARKS AS A KID. FOR NATIVE NEW JER-
seyans, it's basically a tradition to go to Morey's Piers and
Raging Waters Water Park in Wildwood as soon as the
weather is sunny. Until I was about eleven years old, I was
too afraid to ride the roller coasters. I'd choose to go inside
the fun houses instead. The large distorted mirrors would
make me feel like I was an exaggerated version of myself, or
even someone altogether different. The first things to grow
enormously larger were my breasts; then it would be my hips
and finally my butt. I was already a well-endowed kid, so
there wasn't much make-believe there. The fantasy came
from watching little white girls giggle and whisper in each

other's ears as they posed in front of these mirrors, puckering their lips, leaning forward and placing their hands on their knees so that their butts pushed out. Their curvy reflections resembled my female relatives, and these girls loved it. They would laugh at how ridiculous they looked.

And as soon as they walked past the mirrors, they would go back to being stick thin and tall.

The face cutouts were another form of entertainment. I'd see kids, both black and white, whose parents had coaxed them into sticking their heads through the holes so that they could take pictures above the painted bodies on the board. These cutouts were always on top of white bodies. I never participated. Frankly, I thought it looked ridiculous: my black head on top of a white body. It was a deformity that I could not forget about in the land of make-believe. Since my mind couldn't fantasize about this possibility, there was no way I was going to make my body reach a state of being, that being whiteness, if my mind wasn't already there. After the cheerleader incident, that "state" had been marked off with barricade tape. Besides, if I wanted to transform, I was going to do so entirely. Anything less than that was not worth the trouble.

ONE OF MY FONDEST CHILDHOOD MEMORIES IS FROM WHEN I was three years old. It was evening. A group of black women, including my mother, either stood or sat at the table in our kitchen. There was an almost mystical glow emanating from the overhead light. One of my mother's longtime friends put me in a booster seat and, with a thin comb, began to divide my thick hair into sections and slather a white substance on it from the roots to the tips. When I was little, aside from my nose, my hair was the only evidence of my race. I barely had any melanin, and I burned in the sun; I was so much lighter than everyone else in my family and church community that people joked that I was the milkman's baby or the daughter of a white man. But my hair was black, obsidian like ink, and grew into a massive afro.

At first, this application of what I later found out was a perm seemed okay.[1] The product was cool upon my scalp, but then I began to twist and turn in my seat because that coolness turned into tingling and that tingling became a burn. I started to cry. I was immediately taken to the sink, my head placed underneath the faucet. Once the water hit my head, my afro flattened into loose strands that I could see rotating around one other in the stream. My mother's friend ran her fingers through my hair and I hissed, noting how sensitive my scalp had become. What happened next is hazy, but it doesn't really matter because that night began a tradition of more than a decade.

I grew up learning about "good" and "bad" hair. Natural hair was not a style that I saw as a child, unless you count the biracial, light-skinned black girls whose midback- to waist-length curly hair turned bone straight in the pool. I was told that I had "good" hair even though my hair was just as thick, if not thicker, than that of other girls, maybe because I am light-skinned and my complexion somehow mitigated the thickness of my afro.

That white beauty was the ideal was never formally taught

to me. I learned it through warnings and observation. I noticed my white female classmates seemed more invested in the latest lip gloss colors than in their hair. Meanwhile, my eyes and those of my black female classmates surveilled whose hair might be fake, whose hair might be real. If a black girl's hair didn't touch her shoulders, someone might have easily called her "bald-headed" as an insult. If I impulsively wanted to jump in the pool, my mother would tell me, "You're not a white girl, Morgan. You can't just jump in the pool without letting me know." So I began to pay more attention to the white girls I knew who *could* just jump into the pool and reemerge looking like bathing suit models or extras on *Baywatch*. They didn't have to sleep with bonnets or scarves. They rolled their head around on pillows and allowed anyone to play with their tresses.

In the evenings, during Nick at Nite, I watched Marcia Brady of *The Brady Brunch* excessively brushing in front of the vanity mirror in the bedroom she shared with Jan and Cindy. Every day, on my TV, Marcia would wake up, but Carol Brady would never yell from downstairs that she was coming up so that she could do Marcia's hair. That practice was strangely missing, planting one of the first seeds of difference in my head. My hair care regime was much more strenuous, and demanded more of my time, than Marcia's.

The painstaking effort directed towards one's hair is taught incredibly early, and it never lets up. Many mothers choose to plait their daughters' hair to make it grow quicker and then, around grade school age or so, perm it to see its true length. From the age of three to around fifteen, I received a perm every four to six weeks. I started to go to a salon when

I was around eight or nine years old. The hairdresser would apply the perm to my head, and within a matter of minutes, I would complain that it was burning.

"That's okay, it's working," she would always say, and leave the room to take a phone call or eat Chinese or soul food in the sitting area of the salon.

I would clench the handles of my seat and tighten my entire body. My eyes would turn bloodshot, and I could think about nothing else but the pain, which was of a degree that I, to this day, have never experienced in any other situation. I silently repeated to myself, *It's working. It's working. The burning means that it's working.*

That burning didn't just affect my scalp. My skull could feel it, too. Every time I was sure that I was going to be injured, but I tried to soothe myself by imagining how pretty I would be once my hair swished and swayed whenever I walked. As soon as the hairdresser returned, I dashed to the sink and rolled my butt around on the cushion in order to get comfortable. When the water hit my scalp, it stung. Each time the hairdresser worked her fingertips through the back of my head, a new scab would appear, and she would admonish me not to scratch my scalp so much in between sessions; then, she said, it wouldn't burn as much, and new scabs wouldn't appear on my scalp. I took her advice and patted my head whenever I had an itch, but the scabs still appeared. All of the pain disappeared, though, when my hair was finally dried, trimmed, and flat-ironed. I would stand in front of the large mirror wall in the salon sitting area and twirl around and around, beaming at how my strands flew in the current created by my outstretched arms. This, I thought, was how I was supposed to be. Nothing else would do.

I was obsessed not only with my hair's straightness, but also with its length. I thought that if I had long hair, not only would I fulfill my beauty's ultimate potential but I would also elude the restraints of my blackness. I was already mistaken for Dominican and Puerto Rican by Dominicans and Puerto Ricans. Besides the white girls, the Latinas were the most sought after in my school. They were often called sexy or hot, and I began to think that these attributes were inherent to their ethnicity. I watched rap video after rap video of black and Latina women dancing and swimming in pools with their hair flowing past their shoulders (not realizing that many of these styles were lace front wigs and weaves). Long hair would seal the deal for me.

Each time I got my hair permed or braided, I asked the hairdresser to show me the length of my hair before she started. One birthday, my eleventh or twelfth, I wished for hair that stopped underneath my breasts before I blew out the candles on my cake. If straightness would draw me closer to purity, length would draw me closer to sexiness, and stretching between these two poles would make me perfect. At the age of eleven or twelve, I stretched only to undo myself.

Now that I have been natural for almost the same amount of time as I was permed, I can better understand the tremendous amount of duress that both black girls and women put themselves under in order to look "good," whatever that means. The perm is sometimes called "creamy crack," which is quite charged given the racial and socioeconomic context of America's crack epidemic and the War on Drugs. It is a widespread misconception that Madam C. J. Walker, the first female self-made millionaire in America, created the perm. She did build an incredibly successful business around a system of scalp cleansers, massaging methods, and petroleum-based ointment applications that black women could use to combat hair loss due to a previously nonexistent black hair care industry, infrequent bathing, and poor diet, but it was actually Garrett Augustus Morgan, an African-American inventor, who accidentally discovered that the solution he used to ease the friction of sewing machines in his tailor shop also smoothed the nap on fabric and straightened hair. He patented G. A. Morgan Hair Refining Cream and also sold pressing combs and skin bleach.

The root of the word "refined" is "fine," meaning the absence of impurities or blemishes. The Old English root of the word "white" is "*hwit*," meaning "bright, clear, radiant, and fair." As one of the oldest English surnames, it also means "morally pure." The term "white" was first recorded in association with fair complexion in 1600—less than twenty years before the official start of slavery in the North American colonies. In 1852, "white" in American English began to pertain to white people, and in 1868, after the publication of Dr. John H. Van Evrie's *White Supremacy and Negro Subordination*, "white" pertained to not only white people but also their hegemony over nonwhite people. We are taught to straighten our hair because our hair in its natural state deviates from what white people consider acceptable.

An African-American perm, or hair relaxer, is usually made from sodium hydroxide or guanidine hydroxide. (For white people, the main agent for a perm is ammonium thioglycolate, which is considered the mildest of the three chemical straighteners.) Sodium hydroxide contains such a strong chemical base that it can be used to unclog drains and dissolve cellulose fibers from wood and wastepaper. It can cause second or third degree burns in contact with skin, blindness if eyes are exposed, and gastrointestinal damage if ingested. Now imagine this being slathered on a three-year-old child's head. Imagine black mothers consulting dermatologists to see whether they can use relaxer on a one-year-old's head.[2]

You may consider this to be grotesque. In a sense, it is. But the more significant tragedy is that black women are forced to shoehorn themselves into a model of white female beauty. Many of us—myself included—jeopardized our health by not working out because sweat would mess up our perms. Many of us make fiscally bad decisions, skip a bill or two, in order to keep up with regular perms. When we can't get perms, we gel our edges and hair to squeeze it back into the biggest ponytail that we can create. We get the rat-tail comb, we get the wide-tooth comb. We get the paddle brush, we get the bristle brush. We get the flat iron, we get the hot comb. We get the bobby pins, we get the barrettes. We get the small rubber bands, we get the wide rubber bands. We get the sponge hair rollers, we get the plastic hair rollers. We get the bonnets, we get the scarves. We get the plastic caps, we get the wraps. We get the gel, we get the Vaseline. We get the water, we get the grease. We eschew swimming in the pool because chlorine damages our hair. (I haven't swum in over ten years.) If we do get in the pool, we immediately have to wash our hair. We often do not allow others, even black men, to touch our hair. We run our fingers through our hair to see if the naps—or "beadie beads," as we liked to call them—were beginning to grow, which meant another perm was soon to come. Why? Because black women are conscious of how much our appearances are scrutinized, so we painstakingly put ourselves through these beauty rituals to paradoxically create some kind of peace, to "fit in," and therefore be left alone.

We need to consider how we talk about black women's hair. So much cultural scripting happens around our hair, perhaps more than any other place on our bodies. In the 1700s, black women's hair was categorized as wool, which immediately suggests they are more animal than human. In Old English, "shag" meant "matted hair or wool." "Nappy," derived from the word "downy" in the late fifteenth century, is related to "nap," another bed-related activity. The word "nap" was most likely introduced by Flemish cloth workers, but its Old English cognate means "to pluck" and its Gothic cognate means "to tear." Somehow, this term, "nap," which has both sexual and violent implications, became a derogative term for black people's hair in 1950.

"Kinky" means either "full of twists and coils," or "sexually perverted." When we conjure up images of a black woman's hair growing outward, thick and wild, we are unconsciously likening her hair to the imagery and act of sex, with an undertone of force. This is why there are so many examples throughout history of the desire to tame black women's hair in any capacity. Even touch becomes political, a narrative of black women's bodies as spectacles, freak exhibits. It is understandable why a black woman wouldn't allow anyone who is not black to touch her hair because this petting is a form of that fetishization. But what about those who are also black? In Chris Rock's *Good Hair* documentary, an array of black male celebrities express their discontent at not being able to touch a black woman's hair. Many of them admit that they have never touched their partners' hair. Touch is a form of intimacy, and for a black woman, to achieve this kind of connection comes with many challenges.

The significance of black women's hair is nothing new. In many West African cultures, hair possesses a spiritual, aesthetic, and sociocultural importance. During the fifteenth century, many tribes, such as the Wolof, Mende, Mandingo, and Yoruba used hairstyles as a communication system through which they carried messages. The comb was a special implement, too. Men would carve symbols into combs that indicated their religion, family history, and class. As Africans were transported to the New World, their hair became defiled by perspiration, blood, sweat, feces, and urine, and so slave traders shaved their heads, justifying this practice for sanitary reasons. However, many writers and researchers believe it was also intended to dehumanize them and strip them of any legacy from their respective cultures.[3]

When they finally arrived in the New World, Africans had no palm oil, combs, and herbal ointments with which to treat their hair. Instead, they made do with cornmeal and kerosene for scalp cleaners, coffee as a natural dye, and butter to condition. Field slaves especially were not encouraged to invest in hair care, and the women wore scarves for both aesthetic and comfort purposes. But scarves were also enforced as a means of repression. In 1786, Governor Esteban Rodríguez Miró of the then-Spanish provinces of Florida and Louisiana, passed restrictions affecting black women, called the tignon laws. These mandated that women of African descent, either enslaved or free, cover their heads with a knotted headdress so that they would not compete with white women in beauty, dress, and manner, or confuse white men who might otherwise make inappropriate advances towards them.

Over three hundred years later, our culture is still grappling with how to control black women's bodies and identities through their hair. Before 2014, two-strand twists were not accepted in the US Army, Air Force, or Navy. In that same year, both the Army and Air Force decided to remove the words "matted" and "unkempt" from their grooming guidelines. In 2013, the Horizon Science Academy administration in Lorain, Ohio, sent a letter to parents outlining a ban on afro-puffs and small twisted braids. That same year, seven-year-old Tiana Parker of Deborah Brown Community School in Tulsa, Oklahoma, was sent home for having dreadlocks because they did not look "presentable" and would "distract from the respectful and serious atmosphere it strives for." In 2016, the administration of Butler Traditional High School in Louisville, Kentucky, sent home a list of guidelines mandating that hair be kept "clean and neat at all times" and banning dreadlocks, cornrows, and twists because they are "extreme, distracting, or attention-getting."[4]

In pop culture, we don't take kindly to black women

with natural hair. When I was growing up, the only black female characters whom I saw regularly with natural hair were Moesha and Maxine from *Living Single*, although their hair was always styled in braids, not in an afro or twists.[5]

When we straighten our hair with chemical products, we are surrendering to the dominant white culture. We do this to appear more docile; we do this to get jobs, move in and out of various social circles. This is not to say that every woman who gets a perm is subjugating herself. For many it is truly an aesthetic choice.

Around age fifteen, I'd had enough of the creamy crack and so I stopped, cold turkey. I didn't realize until my hair broke off that you cannot quit any drug cold turkey. You have to be weaned off it. I hid my hair's damage with braids, weaves, ponytail clips, and full wigs. I flinch now at photos from that time. My thick hair puffed out from my scalp underneath straight dark brown hair. Anyone could see where my real hair ended and the weave began. In the summer, the difference was far worse. If I flat-ironed the hair left out of the weave, I had to make sure I didn't make too sharp of a movement in windy weather, or engage in too much activity, because my hair would puff out again. I wore wigs that aged me, but at least my hair then was entirely straight, an ideal I was still chasing; I could be less picky about the length. Braids gave me length but not straightness. In both cases, I was never satisfied because I never fully accepted what came naturally out of my own scalp. It was not worth adding onto what brought me shame; no genuine happiness could come from any extension of my hair.

IN THE SUMMER OF 2015, NEWS BROKE THAT RACHEL DOLEZAL, the president of the NAACP Spokane chapter and former professor of Africana studies at Eastern Washington University, had been masquerading as a black woman when she was, in fact, born to two white parents. Dolezal predicated much of her racial identity on outward appearances. She wore bronze foundation and traditionally African-American hairstyles, such as micro braids and kinky wigs, in her effort to "be" a black woman. When asked about her race, Dolezal first said, "I don't understand that question," and in a later interview, she said, "I wouldn't say that I'm African-American, but I would say that I'm black." And then she explained she was "transracial," which is not only bullshit but an insult to people of color who are not afforded the privilege of a malleable identity. I do not condone what Dolezal did. I abhor it, actually. But interestingly enough, she caused me to turn inward, to consider my experiences, my looks, my ideas, and piece together what black womanhood means. And believe me, it is more than naps and brown skin. I may not be able to fully articulate that *thing*, but that's because I've never been asked how and who I imagine myself and other black women to be.

Since slavery, black womanhood has represented the perverse, the grotesque, the ugly. Russian literary critic Mikhail Bakhtin defined a grotesque image as one that is frightening and funny at the same time, and there is no more acute example of this than Hottentot Venus, whose large body was a source of entertainment for white people.

Born in 1789 in South Africa's Eastern Cape, Sara "Saartjie" Baartman experienced great hardship at a young age.

Both of her parents died before she reached adulthood, her fiancé was murdered by Dutch colonists, and her child also died. Because Baartman had steatopygia, or extremely large buttocks, she drew the attention of Hendrik Cesars, in whose house she worked as a servant, and Englishman William Dunlop, who sought to capitalize on her body. Legend has it that although Baartman was illiterate, she signed a contract that she would travel with both Cesars and Dunlop to Europe in order to participate in shows. Promoters nicknamed her "Hottentot Venus," "hottentot" being a derogative term used by the Dutch towards the Khoisan people, an indigenous group of Southern Africa. Besides gawking at her onstage, wealthy people could pay for private exhibitions of her in their homes where they were allowed to touch her. After Baartman died at twenty-six, naturalist Georges Cuvier not only preserved her skeleton, but also pickled her brain and genitals, containing them in jars and displaying them at Paris's Museum of Man. They remained there until 1974.

We as black women are not afforded ownership over our own identities, our own bodies, the color of our skin and the texture of our hair, and yet white women can appropriate our bodies in order to suit their own selfish desires. bell hooks writes in "Eating the Other" that ". . . ethnicity becomes spice, seasoning that can liven up the dull dish that is mainstream white culture." White women's privilege allows them to do this with little, if any, reproach.

That black women's bodies are problematic manifests in several flash points, such as hair, but when embodied by white women these flash points are neutralized, even admired. Case in point: *Marie Claire* praised Kylie Jenner's "epic" cornrows while black women are still discriminated against in the workplace for wearing such a hairstyle. In February 2013, the international fashion magazine *Numéro* did an editorial spread called "African Queen," in which the lily-white model Ondria Hardin was in blackface. Black skin and hair are considered "epic" and regal as long as they are not found on the black female body, because that kind of authenticity is not the kind of beauty that mainstream culture values. A simple Google search for "beautiful women" reveals a proliferation of white women.

Some may ask how we can demonize Dolezal when black women try to "look white," with weaves that look nothing like their natural hair texture, or blue contacts. The answer is that when there is no equality, there cannot be equivalency. In other words, we cannot judge black and white women in the same way. Although black women are pressured to be as close to the white ideal as possible, they can never call themselves white. There are benefits to looking "respectable"—a chance at getting certain jobs, moving in and out of elite circles, vast networks, and so on—but like a black child who places her face through a cutout on top of a white body at a carnival or amusement park, a black woman with a Russian weave and baby-blue contacts will never be viewed as a white woman. She will be seen as a black woman with a Russian weave and baby-blue contacts. We all know that we cannot identify as something that we can never inherently be.

Dolezal, on the other hand, managed to embody whiteness, white womanhood, in the guise of black womanhood. Only a white woman could pose as a black woman and not be immediately laughed out of town. Rachel Dolezal's massive media blitz after she was "outed," everywhere from MSNBC to *Vanity Fair*, was no accident. Although Dolezal darkened her skin, she still inhabits a white female body and, as such, possesses the privilege to take black female characteristics and subsequently become a newsworthy subject. While actual black women are stigmatized for the bodies that we live in, when Rachel Dolezal attempts to wear our bodies as a kind of costume, she becomes intellectualized. Only a white woman could inspire others to discuss if races can be switched, and when someone like Rachel Dolezal does so, she is protected—even defended. It is true that she was also condemned and mocked, but this backlash was followed with a book deal and massive press junket, not obscurity. Dolezal is not an innovator. She's just carrying on tradition. In the late nineteenth century, white women wore bustles to make their buttocks look bigger than they were. Hottentot Venus influenced this style, and yet what was natural on her was seen as disgusting; what was artificial on white women was seen as a sign of luxury. The offense does not lie only in the imitation itself, but also in the reception of black women's body parts, which are only coveted once a white woman decides that she wants them for herself. Black women cannot reappropriate from white women and be equally desired. White women are not pressured to look like anyone else but themselves. Yet when they want to look like black women, they still are seen as both original and acceptable. Under the white gaze, the black body cannot exist without white people encroaching upon our right to be. We are like bendy straws, able to curve and snap depending on a white person's curiosity. We are not black "people" on our own, but rather the opposite of whiteness. I am beyond questioning if all of this is mere coincidence. Because of history and current pop culture references, it seems as if it's all by design, which makes the discussions around beauty—who gets to own and determine it—very difficult and painful.

WHEN I WAS GROWING UP, EVERY BLACK GIRL I KNEW HAD A Barbie—a blonde-haired, blue-eyed, perfect-white-woman prototype. I hated dolls; their still eyes made me feel like I was always being watched, and I much preferred stuffed animals. Still, I saw girls carrying Barbie everywhere because Barbie was a hot commodity back then. But even more than that, she was a status symbol: a small piece of white luxury available for purchase. If you bought her, you, too, could share in that counterfeit ideal. Why do you think you don't see many white girls with black dolls? I saw a video online of two white girls having a fit when they received black dolls for Christmas. Black dolls don't represent beauty, luxury, and perfection. These things are for white girls, not black girls.

Like the girls I grew up with, Claudia MacTeer in Toni Morrison's *The Bluest Eye* treasures a "blue-eyed, yellow-haired, pink-skinned doll." The possession of one, as she says, is what every little girl in the world, whether she be black or white, wants. Black and white girls want the same white doll. Only problem is, white girls stare at Barbies and see potential. Black girls stare at white dolls and see impossibility. This is what stirs Claudia to ask, "What made people look at them and say, 'Awwwww,' but not for me?" Her quandary can only be solved if she destroys a white doll, a symbol of white womanhood. White women can weave magic around others in a way that she cannot.

In our patriarchal culture, both white and black women have to fight for the reclamation of their bodies. But we cannot group all women together under the patriarchy without considering race, which further stigmatizes us as black women but provides a buffer for white women.

Their womanhood does not eliminate their whiteness. We as black women are doubly disenfranchised in the throes of two spaces, race and gender, and there is no solace. Toni Morrison once said that "the black woman has nothing to fall back on: not maleness, not whiteness, not ladyhood, not anything. And out of the profound desolation of her reality, she may very well have invented herself." Morrison's predecessor Zora Neale Hurston wrote in *Their Eyes Were Watching God* that black women are "de mule uh de world." The offspring of a male donkey and a female horse, a mule is not quite one, not quite the other. Mules require less sustenance and support than horses. Their hooves are much harder, which helps to ward off disease and infection, and they have thicker skin. Black women, like mules, have always had much less support and a greater burden. And our efforts rarely receive acknowledgment; if they do, it is only as footnotes on our cultural narrative. This is why the idea of the Strong Black Woman is sweet in sound but damaging in effect.

Lorraine Bethel, a black lesbian feminist poet, wrote a poem called "What Chou Mean *We*, White Girl?" about buying a sweater that was once owned by a white woman. When Bethel smells the sweater, its scent is comfort, a delicacy that she will never know in her life. This comfort that

Bethel describes is one that I believe black women secretly desire, but also eschew. There is pride in getting by with less. We do it, our mothers have done it, and our female ancestors have surely done it, too. There is a pride in still being here *in spite of it all*, and that's a feeling that white women will never be able to experience. But even though black women may not want to be white women, "frustration" and "anger" would be plausible words for how some of us may feel about all the benefits of their whiteness that they receive— luxuries won without any exhaustion, without an investment of labor. We never had organized groups like the KKK believing so strongly in our purity that they would lynch any sun-kissed man for even looking in our direction. We are never in mainstream spaces without someone asking, *Why?* With white women it's, *Why not?* Our existence begs more questioning. Their existence doesn't and, in fact, often comes with praise for just having shown up. We are afterthoughts; they are the nuclei. White women have been the basis of feminism, and they have fought for their rights at the expense of black people. Elizabeth Cady Stanton once asserted, "The representative women of the nation have done their uttermost for the last thirty years to secure freedom for the Negro . . . but now, as the celestial gate to civil rights is slowly moving on its hinges, it becomes a serious question whether we had better stand aside and see 'Sambo' walk into the kingdom first . . ."

And arguably, white women have a vested interest in a patriarchy that is more ruinous towards black women's bodies than their own. Our pussies do not unite us. It is easy for white people, especially women, to cut away at our bodies like we are meat on a slab. It was easy for nineteenth-century white women to wear bustles to make their asses look bigger; easy for Rachel Dolezal to slap on a wig and brown foundation and call herself black; easy for Kylie to wear cornrows and be seen as an innovator. We are not seen as people, but rather as parts that can be appropriated and tailored anytime and in any place.

When black women look at Rachel Dolezal, we see someone who used our skin and hair as a cloak. She never lived in a black woman's body, because if she did she'd know that to be like us is to always dwell in a place of war. Our bodies are vulnerable; we await attack as we salt our wounds from the last one. We are the mules whose origins we cannot fully imagine, but now is our time to reclaim our dreams about ourselves. What is the black woman, and how do we go about procuring this knowledge about who she is? We've been finding out who we are through the influence that we have upon everyone else and the influence they have on us. Black men, white men, white women—each one of these groups has had a stake in our bodies, even though we've never given our consent. We have to get our bodies back somehow, but we must navigate our own bodies first. How do we turn inward? How do we find a place of refuge within them?

I've never been asked what I am in my own imagination. What is a black woman to herself out from under the shadow of the white woman? For black women, whiteness and white womanhood linger over our heads, smothering our consciousness every day. But we are not the inverse of whiteness—or white womanhood, for that matter. Still our bodies find a way to come back to us distorted like images in fun house mirrors. We know something is wrong with the distortions, but we cannot say what. This is the magic that I believe Claudia talks about in *The Bluest Eye*. But if we are not the opposite of whiteness, then what are we? Maybe the truth is that we are invisible to ourselves. The truth is, we are all clamoring for something ancient within our souls that is still virgin from white touch. We are nostalgic for something that we cannot claim, an artifact within ourselves that was not chained when our foremothers were transported across the Atlantic to the New World. The Portuguese call this "*saudade,*" feeling a loss or absence of something that we know will never return.

We may never find it, but we must keep digging anyhow. It is an arduous battle to piece together our existence while we are trying to resist during our individual lives. I do believe in the Audre Lorde saying that you cannot dismantle the master's house with the master's tools. But we've been working in that house for centuries. We may know the tools better than the master, and we must know all the ways in which they operate in order to destroy the master's power over our lives. We must consider white womanhood. If we abandon that prematurely without studying its influence, then we will not know all the ways in which that power functions so that we can trap it before it traps us. But we must not dwell on it for too long. For as long as white women have been appropriating our bodies, we have been insulted and afflicted. And frankly, I am tired of being in such an abusive relationship that I never agreed to in the first place. There was never any honeymoon period. There is no need to consider those who take without giving, speak without listening, and use feminism as a way to unify without analyzing black women's differences and their complications.

I HAD NO DESIRE TO SEE MY NATURAL HAIR UNTIL I WENT TO Princeton and I saw many black women abandon the creamy crack and hot comb. Maybe it was due to a lack of sufficient funds or black hair stylists around the area, but nevertheless, I was inspired. One evening, two of my closest friends helped me to undo my Senegalese twists and wash my hair. Once the water hit my scalp, my strands did not rotate around one other in the stream. Instead they transformed into tight coils whose definition could only be seen if they were separated from one another with the use of hands or cream that consisted not of sodium hydroxide but shea butter, jojoba oil, coconut oil, aloe vera juice, and avocado oil, among other things. There was no pain, no burn. I stared at myself in the mirror, afraid to touch my own curls out of fear that they would snap off in my hands. I felt naked, unsure of my own natural beauty.

I went to a dorm party later that evening, and there I received more compliments than I ever had with any other style. At first, I was confused. I wondered if people were just being nice because they knew I was deathly insecure and they wanted to make me feel better about my hot mess of a hairdo. My afro barely touched my shoulders. How could anyone consider this beautiful? But they did. I will never forget the increased breadth of sensation I experienced when

I walked out of my dormitory and felt the undulations of the wind coursing through my scalp. I didn't have to worry about when I would need to schedule my next perm because the wind had gotten the best of my style. I'll never forget how self-conscious I felt walking from one end of an Ivy League campus to the other, worried that I would feel less deserving than I already did. But damn, did it feel good to be free.

When my mother found out about my natural hair, she worried that my hair would break off because I wouldn't be able to take care of it. So I watched YouTube video after YouTube video on how to moisturize, preshampoo, wash, deep-condition, and create two-strand twists. When I washed my hair with SheaMoisture products while showering and stepped out to return to the mirror, I did not immediately grab a towel to cover my body. Instead, I watched my hair spiral into tight coils again, the water hiding in and around my scalp, and I became aroused. I thought maybe this was because I was naked and watching water bead down the hills of my breasts, but I was looking only at my hair. For years, I had complied with a tradition and restrained my sexuality, the appeal of my hair, through perms and relaxers and hot combs. But this place, more than any other site on my body, was the domain of my humanity.

And if I step away from the mirror altogether, I can really look at myself: my skin, my large afro, and my curvy frame. The realization of who I am is more visceral. I look down at my thick thighs and my large breasts, and I know that I have this body. This body is mine and I hold on to it. I want to know how I exist in my own imagination. The black female imaginary is what happens when you see yourself as another black woman may see you. The black female imaginary is what happens when you look at yourself, when your body is what you hold on to and your mind focuses inward to inquire about who you are, not outward to actively combat what is out *there*. I know that as a black woman, I am a problem. I am a contradiction of what it means to be human, but I am still here anyhow. I speak, I talk, I think, and I walk with a swivel in my hips. Perhaps it is the black female imaginary and not whiteness that is strange and mysterious, but I prefer it to be that way. When I see other black women whose behavior and decision making towards their appearances I cannot understand, I know the parts I'm searching for in me are already in them and vice versa. We need to collect our many imaginations together in order to build a body of knowledge. We are fighting just by living.

I have been natural for over ten years now. My hair is longer than it's ever been. Defining my curls takes a concerted effort. My afro is thick. My shrinkage is massive, although I prefer it this way. My hair holds much more than it ever has, and I feel like I am living who I really am. Rubbing coconut oil or shea butter into my curls becomes a meditative process, a way in which to maintain my beauty. If my hair is considered wild, so be it. I prefer it that way. Thankfully, a huge natural hair movement is happening. Many natural hair bloggers, video content makers, and even regular black women are emerging in our culture, so the dichotomized images of black hair are becoming less so.

Sexuality is harnessed through black women's manes. Its wildness and expansiveness is a sight to behold. It is something that many institutions try to tame but cannot. And I, for one, enjoy living my life as a provocation.

I am who I am despite imposters, despite the carnivalesque images of my body reflected back at me by our society. I am a stranger and I like it.

4

A HUNGER FOR MEN'S EYES

But if they cannot contain, let them marry: for it is better to marry than to burn.
—1 Corinthians 7:9 KJV

When I was a child, I held in my head a concrete image of marrying at twenty-two. It seemed to me then like the perfect age because I would be finished with college, and I'd figured that women were over the hill by the age of twenty-five. On my mother's side of the family, the oldest member, male or female, to get married had been twenty-six. My grandmother married at sixteen and my mother at seventeen. They had children less than two years into their marriages. I assumed that I would follow in their footsteps, not only because there was a clear pattern but also because I did not know how long I would be able to contain myself.

Aside from being off the mark about when a woman should reach personal milestones, unsurprisingly, I also had no idea what marriage entailed. I'd never envisioned a wedding gown, the exchange of rings, a first dance. I just imagined infinite kisses and bodies pressed together, the stuff I saw in R-rated movies when I was around twelve or thirteen. What exactly those bodies did, I wasn't sure, but I knew it had to be good since neither party wanted to pull away. I was raised not to explore my sexuality with an unfettered curiosity unless it was set within the parameters of marriage. I believed that as long as I had a diamond ring encircling my finger, I would be in the clear.

I WAS AROUND ELEVEN YEARS OLD, AND IT WAS SUMMER. I was spending time at one of my cousins' homes in South Jersey. Another cousin, Mia, who was only a couple years older than I was and whom I saw about once a year whenever her mom decided to come into town from Ohio, joined me in one of the spare rooms, where I was changing into my bathing suit to meet the rest of my family in the pool. I do not remember how we got on the topic of breasts, but I suppose it was because mine were either exposed or spilling over the cups of my bra because I was a 34C before I was in the sixth grade. Surprised, Mia commented on how big I was, and I nervously half smiled as I always did whenever these remarks were directed towards me.

And then she asked me, "You aren't scared?"

I jerked my neck and asked, "Scared? Scared of what?"

The tone of her voice shifted and her reply sounded like a whine. "When I go back to school, I have to worry because the guys in my year pinch the boobs of any girl they see and I'm next."

When I looked at Mia, however, I was surprised that she didn't look terrified, but instead she seemed sort of annoyed, sort of excited. Her eyes were downcast, but her lips were upturned. I do not know if she was smiling to ease the tension. She was a mess of contradiction; I'd actually heard a note of fear and resignation.

"Can't you tell someone if they do it to you?" I naively asked.

"It doesn't matter. They gon' do it anyway."

There was nothing more to say and we finished changing.

I forgot about Mia's words until I began sixth grade. The racial hierarchies of male desire were much more apparent that year. At the top there were the white girls, whom every boy wanted. White girls were always considered the most beautiful and popular, but they were mostly out of reach. Latinas were beautiful and popular, too, but more accessible; the boys considered them more sexually mature. Anyone of Asian descent was on the margins. As for the black girls, if you were not light-skinned, you were automatically considered the least attractive. It wasn't unusual for me to hear dark-skinned black girls called "burnt," as if they should be discarded because they'd been left on the heat for too long.

My male classmates openly competed to see how many butts they could slap at recess. Only the Latinas and black girls were targets. Sometimes, I would see girls looking over their shoulders and subsequently running away, smiling, before boys caught up with them to smack their butts and then run in the opposite direction. If a girl was slapped, she rarely got upset because at least she was considered attractive enough to slap. She was being watched, a guy just *had* to touch her, and who didn't want that?

I was anxious about when I would get slapped. I had a crush on a guy named Juan, a Puerto Rican classmate with intense eyes and a suaveness that far surpassed his years. Although I had known him to exclusively date white girls, when he was single his arms would be like windmills, winding up and rolling around to see who he could slap. His hands were quicker than his friends', and while they often almost got caught by the teachers within a millisecond, Juan always went undetected. I spent countless days fantasizing about when he would choose me to be his girlfriend, or at least say that I was pretty. But as time passed, my hope diminished. So I went for another approach: I wanted to learn how to be cooler. My rapidly growing rapport with a group of black girls could not have come at a better time. Two of them, Kiki and Bethany, had a kind of wit I desperately desired. Every recess, they taught me how to walk while rolling my hips, and they stood on each side of me as I practiced. They watched my jaw whenever I spoke and made me loosen it, to let the words flow and slur together on their own. They critiqued my laugh so that it no longer reached a higher octave but stayed consistent, my chuckles flittering until my diaphragm almost gave out. Finally, I had to become stylish, the hardest achievement of all. Instead of wearing Limited Too and Gap, I wanted Apple Bottom jeans, Baby Phat T-shirts, Timbs, and fitted hats. The Holy Grail was a jersey dress. A jersey dress was tight enough to accentuate curves, long enough to avoid a trip to the principal's office, and short enough to make a guy notice all that you were working with.

I purchased a UNC–Chapel Hill jersey dress when I went on vacation with one of my friends and refused to wear it until I returned to school post–spring break. When I pulled the dress over my head and walked to the bus stop, I quietly began to panic. I could not swish my hips in that dress. If I did, I was sure someone would catch a glimpse of my panties. How could I laugh and talk how they'd taught me when I was worried that I could be exposed at any moment? Throughout the morning, I kept my books over my pelvic area and secretly patted my backside behind corners to make sure that I was still protected. At recess, both Kiki and Bethany praised my outfit, and I embellished the story of a ten-minute splurge at an Orlando mall and made it sound like an epic adventure.

Once the whistle was blown, the signal for us to gather into single-file lines, I saw that Juan and his friends were the last to regroup with our class. Before I wouldn't have dared pay him mind, but this day was different; today I was wearing a jersey dress. He had to see me now. The jersey dress was the equivalent of a blinking neon sign, saying, *Woo-hoo, over here.* I glanced over my shoulder as we walked back into the building, our lines dispersing into the usual friend circles. I glanced over my shoulder again and saw that Juan and his friends were looking at me. One raised his eyebrows, another smiled, the other nodded. I smiled and kept walking but slowed my feet. Then suddenly, I felt a light wind and a hard smack landed on my butt. When I turned, I saw that it was Juan. I sucked my teeth and feigned offense and took my seat.

Juan never ended up being my boyfriend. He got back together with his ex, Casey, a white girl with dirty-blonde hair and blue eyes. She was one of the cheerleaders I sucked up to during tryouts, and she made the team every year. She could have had anyone in the school. She knew it, too.

AROUND THAT TIME, MY MOTHER EXPRESSED HER CONCERN about how I was dressing and the girls I'd decided to be-friend. It wasn't the clothes themselves but rather the brands and what kind of impressions they gave to others. She did not want me becoming a "fast-tailed girl" because that was *not who I was*. That was *not who she raised me to be*. Her voice was clear, her eyes unwavering, and she didn't smile. This was not a joke, but a message that I needed to heed for as long as I lived on this earth in this body. I might have heard about the dangers of "fast-tailed girls" before, but this was different because the warning was directed at me. I sat still in quiet submission and then left her bedroom more confused than before, desire and propriety battling within me. Years later, when I read Zadie Smith's novel *Swing Time*, I realized that these sexual childhood games are not limited to America, but are a problem for young black girls across the globe. In the novel, the unnamed British narrator details the tradition of black girls being cornered by their male classmates, who would push their panties aside and stick as many fingers in-side their vaginas as they could. The white girls were not a part of the game. The narrator does not say why, but I know why. It is the same reason why the white girls at my middle school did not get slapped on the butts while the black girls and the Latinas were open territory. I love that Smith chooses not to openly articulate this, because doing so would present an issue for which black girls and women have yet to find its origins.

I do not know where I first encountered the phrase "fast-tailed girl." My mother doesn't either. It is always used by older generations, as it was used by the older generations before them. I've heard it spoken most by black Christian women, and men use it from time to time. "Sluts" or "whores" are terms used more in white spaces; black girls are "fast-tailed" or "ho(e)s." A "fast-tailed girl" may be a black girl who wants attention from men, gets pregnant out of wedlock, spends too much time talking to boys, wears dresses or skirts that are too short, crosses one leg over the other with too much thigh showing during this rearrangement, et cetera, et cetera. It would be wrong to unilaterally categorize this phrase as slut-shaming. On one level, it is. On another level, though, "fast-tailed girl" is a weaponized phrase intended to protect black girls, although its impact tends to be the opposite.

Only black women know black girlhood well enough to understand that once a black baby girl exits the womb, it is not enough that she is alive and well. Even before she's born, folks want to know whether she will be light- or dark-skinned, have good curly hair or a thick afro, share her father's big lips or have her mother's big nose. All of these cultural burdens weigh down her body before she is fully formed. Once she is brought into this world, everyone silently acknowledges the battles that she will fight just for being born a black girl. She cannot just be *good*; she has to be *better* than good in order to meet the white female standard. This black girl cannot just be *presentable* in terms of hair and style; she has to be *acceptable*. She cannot just be *conservative* in terms of sexuality; she has to be *closed off*. Black girls are not afforded the luxury of just being girls. They are never innocent or cute. If only a black girl can be a "fast-tailed girl," then she is not a girl at all, but a beast.

There is no male equivalent for a "fast-tailed girl" within the black community because male sexuality is not only encouraged but praised. Boys are boys, and men are men. Female elders may purse their lips and speak about a black boy's player ways with the ladies, but he is not admonished for being *potentially* promiscuous like black girls are. When he is criticized for his dress, if his pants sag, it is not because this means that his dick is accessible to anyone, or that he is a sexual deviant. He is criticized for his dress because no one wants anyone to assume that he is a lazy good-for-nothing person. No one worries if he's talking too much to girls; in fact, this may even instill pride in his father (though his mother may worry about an unexpected pregnancy). Black girls, however, are oftentimes treated as outsiders inside black spaces.

EVEN THOUGH NEITHER MY GRANDMOTHER NOR MY MOTHER graduated from college, they bought into the general cultural narrative that college is where American women are supposed to find their husbands. I never got into a relationship in high school, for fear of being academically distracted, and so they felt that Princeton was my time to find love. But my mother assumed that because I was entering into an extremely white institution, I would most likely *not* marry someone black. Furthermore, black women outnumbered black men almost three to one at Princeton, and black Americans were the minority compared to the number of Africans and West Indians. I was always open to dating a man of any race, but I first wanted to prove her wrong by any means necessary. I suppose I was less concerned with matters of love and more concerned with showing myself and my mother that I was not unattractive to men of my own community. But when I got there, I soon realized the challenges that I faced.

I joined the Princeton Association of Black Women, and one of our recurring conversations was about our dateability on campus. Mostly we were not in relationships, and this was not out of choice. We all knew that black women were much more likely to remain unmarried compared to white women. We all idolized Michelle Obama for being able to find her equal, even if she hadn't met Barack until well after her undergraduate years. When I was a junior, I successfully "bickered" Cannon, one of Princeton's eleven eating clubs, which was mostly populated by the university's top athletes. Because the eating club system was the center of campus social life, and because I hadn't previously been successful finding my place within it, I felt validated and aimed to take advantage of my new status by trying much harder at parties to be "seen" so that I could leave Princeton saying that I was in at least *one* relationship.

Although I attended Cannon's parties every once in a

while, downing vodka and tequila while wearing crop tops, my drunken confidence did not entice any guy to come my way. I realized just how unattractive I was when, one night while I was sitting in Cannon's main living room lamenting to another black female Cannon member about my frustration at being single, one of the black football players sat down beside us. I considered him a friend. In fact, he was one of the reasons why I'd gotten into Cannon in the first place. But when he got comfortable on the sofa, he needed our help. He and the rest of his teammates were making a list of the most attractive black women at Princeton, and he then proceeded to list a Who's Who of those in my class, asking me to fill in the blanks. I was not among them and I was too afraid to ask why. At that point, it didn't matter. I was invisible to the men I wanted most to attract. I felt like I was an untouchable, at the bottom of our caste system, destined to be both unloved and unsexed.

It didn't help that just weeks before this incident, I had been stood up by a black grad student in the Neuroscience Department, despite the fact that he'd pursued me on a crowded, poorly lit dance floor at a party and asked for my number. We'd hung out at the Woodrow Wilson "Woody Woo" fountain right in front of the Woodrow Wilson School of Public and International Affairs and talked about music and our family lives. He wanted us to see a Broadway show together, and to break me out of my fear of watching scary movies. I wanted him to be mine. He was good-looking enough and talkative, and that seemed adequate.

Our seeing each other lasted two weeks. He never gave a reason for standing me up, only asked to reschedule, which we never did. I remember passing by him in the gym as he quickly averted his eyes. I had grown accustomed to situations like these that had no closure: there was the guy who'd wanted to get dinner in the dining hall, suggested we do it again sometime, then told me he was too busy because he had to work on study abroad applications, only for me to later find out that he wanted to party on a Saturday night with all the girls who were on my football player friend's list. I began to wonder if something was intrinsically wrong with me, something less obvious than a deficit in looks, style, or personality. I thought that I was suffering from some kind of invisible disease and all the men knew it, which is why they quickly abandoned me. Whether it was the desperation oozing through my pores, or a lack of confidence that wore me better than my own clothes, I felt like less of a woman.

At Princeton, I spent a significant amount of my time outside of classrooms and libraries at weekly Bible study meetings, where the fear of being single for too long trickled in. Our coordinator did her best to calm our fears by reiterating that patience was a godly virtue and that, according to the book of Proverbs, we were supposed to be pursued and not vice versa. She'd enjoyed an incredibly harmonious and happy marriage since twenty-two, which is what I wanted, but I wasn't sure that she knew of heartbreak like mine. I wanted to believe her. But I could not be passive. I have always been a driven, outspoken person, and I was known on campus for my fiery debating style and my provocative articles as an opinion columnist for the *Daily Princetonian*.

Suddenly, I started to wonder if this was the reason why I was undesirable: I talked too much, and didn't know how to be docile. Most of the other black women who never seemed to have a shortage of men in pursuit were not as vocal as I was. They seemed less loud, more reserved, and more relaxed in party settings. But by the time I realized this, I was on the verge of graduating and it seemed too late. I had dreamed of marrying at twenty-two, but I had never imagined that I might leave college without ever having been in a relationship or having kissed someone throughout the duration of those four years.

AT TWENTY-TWO, I WAS TRYING TO HAVE A MONOGAMOUS relationship with a man named Bradley, a childhood friend and longtime admirer whom I hadn't spoken to since senior year of high school. I thought I was in love, and I hoped to marry him someday.

He lived and studied thousands of miles away from me, but to my surprise and delight, about three months before graduation, I received a text from him. I thought that he was reaching out just to say hello, but then he invited me on an all-expenses-paid trip to Nevada so we could catch up with each other. I didn't hesitate. I yearned for male attention, and I was afraid that my four-year dry spell at Princeton was steadily turning me cold, bitter, and emotionally mute. For the several weeks leading up to the trip, we spoke every evening. We spoke so often, I felt like he was right beside me. As I descended the escalator at McCarran Airport, I saw Bradley—now several inches taller and wider with muscle— standing there with a bouquet of roses. All of the years of loneliness and rejection melted away as we cruised down the highway in his silver Porsche. When we were children, I'd constantly rebuffed this man's advances, but now that we were adults I was ready. Except that Bradley expected us to have sex, but much to his chagrin I said no because we were not in a committed relationship. It also helped that I got my period on my connecting flight to Nevada. To this day, I believe this buffer was an act of God, signaling to me that the time was not right and he was not it.

Nevertheless, these excuses led to an argument, and he turned away from me in the bed that we shared. He told me that because he was in the military, he received very little physical contact and that was his way to connect. All of this seemed quite plausible, but I still wouldn't budge. I planned on remaining a virgin until marriage, but I was trying to convince myself to settle for a committed relationship—it would be a way to make him stay. I cried in that bed and I wiped my tears without him so much as touching my back. He told me that he didn't want to see me cry and that was that. The next morning, I woke him up, asked him to get a condom, and then I went down on him. It was the most emotionless thing I've ever done. I performed fellatio not because I wanted to but because I thought I had to. He'd spent thousands of dollars on me. He was going to be successful and could have had any woman he wanted. I, who was so unsure of myself, had no job prospects after college and needed a reminder that something was not wrong with me, that I could be wanted. I wasn't going to allow him to penetrate me, but I was going to allow him to be in my mouth for a short while. After all, I thought, it was my mouth that dissuaded men from dating me anyway. I talked too much and gave my opinions too freely. My silence through giving head was my kind of docility. It wasn't supposed to be pleasurable. It was my duty, my debt.

When I returned to New Jersey, I was terrified that he would never reach out to me again. I'd already found a man who was willing to chase me; why couldn't I have been more docile by losing my virginity to him? But then he texted, and in a matter of weeks we'd said we loved each other and were planning a future together. Separated by thousands of miles and state lines, we tried our best to maintain intimacy through frequent video conversations during which we would get naked, and I would watch him climax. I never did because I had no idea what to do to myself. I assumed that if I squeezed my breasts and he orgasmed, then somehow his pleasure would be transmitted through the computer screen and disperse across all my erogenous zones. One night, he asked me if I wanted to watch porn with him. It wasn't like I had never seen it before. I had inadvertently watched a few minutes of porn when I was a child, at the Peninsula hotel in New York City. I remember a guy waving a fleshy wand in between his legs; I was too young to understand that was his penis. When I got older, I used to watch soft-core porn late at night if I was bored, but I never touched myself, figuring that the voyeurism was enough. So when Bradley was enough of a gentleman to ask me to pick a clip out of thousands (or millions), my pointer grazed over random ones: "Asian housemaid gets taught a lesson," "Ebony double stuffed," "Blonde slut gets manhandled." But the one that most piqued my interest was double penetration. Bradley could not understand why any of that would excite me. I couldn't articulate why. He didn't get off while we watched, so I allowed him to switch to something else, but the memory of watching a woman getting filled in three orifices at once, wondering how that was at all possible, flickered behind my eyes. I did the responsible thing and got on birth control. The plan was for me to fly back out to Nevada during the Fourth of July weekend, where we'd have sex and, I guess, ride off into the proverbial sunset.

A week before I was supposed to leave, my mother texted me and asked if it was okay to talk. I was in the middle of my first MFA residency, which I began immediately after graduation, and I knew this had to be serious. When we finally connected, she told me that she had been praying for Bradley and me, and she wanted me to make sure that he really loved me before I decided to be intimate with him. At first I was upset, interpreting her concern as an intentional effort to thwart me on my road to true and everlasting love. But out of respect, I allowed her to finish, and then together we prayed that anything hidden would be revealed. That night, as always, Bradley and I talked for hours. I happened to mention how glad I was that we were finally in a relationship that made me feel secure enough to fly out to see him and have sex, but Bradley was caught off guard. He told me that although he loved me, he was not ready to be in an exclusive relationship. He then went on to say that he thought I was enough for him, but in order for him to be *sure*, he had to experience some things. He still wanted to travel the world and sleep with other women. When I told him that I had waited too long to lose my virginity in such a noncommittal way, we ultimately decided that for me to fly back out to Nevada would not be in my best interest, and we stopped speaking.

Calling what I experienced after our demise "heartbreak" would be an offense to the depth of my feelings. I didn't just break. I shattered. I cried whenever someone uttered his name. I kept my cell phone by my face at night, hoping that I'd hear the buzz of a notification and it would be a message from him telling me how much he missed and loved me. Because I did not immediately get a job out of college, I had moved back home and my idleness worsened my suffering. When I wasn't pitching articles, I was losing myself to grief. I went to two therapy sessions with two different professionals. I took ballroom dancing lessons. I wrote Bradley a letter where I confessed that I thought I was never good enough for him and he responded thanking me for my vulnerability, but sticking to his belief that he had made the right decision.

In retrospect, I know that losing my virginity to Bradley would have been excruciating because I would have felt coerced and judged myself for not feeling aroused. But back then, I hated myself for thinking that my pussy was any better than those of the billions of other women out there who have healthy and happy sex lives with imperfect yet good men like Bradley—with or without commitment.

IT TOOK ME SIX MONTHS TO GO OUT ON A DATE AGAIN AFTER Bradley, a year to get over him, and two years to recover from the pain. Since I spent most of my time indoors, either at my mother's house or in a dancing studio, I decided that the only way I would meet men was OkCupid. Within a few short weeks, I'd connected with a guy named Chris, a redheaded veterinary student at the University of Pennsylvania. On our first date we went to the Cheesecake Factory and then a bar, where we discussed our families, political views, and past dating experiences for two and a half hours. He tried to compliment me by saying that he would date any woman irrespective of race, and that when he saw my profile he didn't see a black woman. I remembered how my outspokenness had perhaps ruined my dating life at college. It was already bad enough that I could not attract black men, and so I kept quiet, afraid to correct Chris about the impossibility of color blindness because he might have mistaken that for aggression. I didn't want to be a black female stereotype, the Sapphire who emasculates men and usurps their dominant role.

Since the 1800s, one of the stereotypes that black women in popular culture fall into is that of the "sassy mammies." Because they were accepted in white families, their presence gave the impression that their oppression was minimal. The name "Sapphire" came from Sapphire Stevens, an *Amos 'n' Andy* character, who constantly mocked her husband, Kingfish, leader of a black fraternal lodge in Harlem, calling him a failure. Both black and nonblack men know the Sapphire very well. She's Hattie McDaniel in *Gone with the Wind*, Tracy Jordan's wife in *30 Rock*, Omarosa Manigault on *The Apprentice*: any loud neck- and eye-rolling black woman who dares to challenge a man or voice her opinion. Black women aren't presented as people to be loved, but rather as sources of entertainment, and black women's mouths are always a spectacle.

I thought that I would only be seen as desirable, as a real woman, if I kept quiet. Within a span of a few seconds, from the time Chris lifted his drink to when he sipped it, I tried to teach myself how to be silent and allow a man to speak even if what he said was wrong. No person, especially not a woman, should do this because it's impossible, and demeaning to try. But what was I supposed to do: Ruin a good evening by defending myself? Perhaps I was overthinking it.

In retrospect, I know that I was thinking just the right amount. Chris didn't see me as a "black woman" because he didn't want to see me as one. It was easy for him to make this judgment when I was just a 400×600 image online, unmoving and unspeaking. But it could've been worse, I thought. He could have called me a nigger or exoticized me, which only demonstrates how low my standards were for white men at the time. He concluded the night by kissing me on the cheek and asking to schedule our next date, so I assumed that my silence had worked to my advantage. The next time we met, we went to an Indian restaurant and then another bar, and we kissed on the lips before parting ways. Then I didn't hear anything from him, and I grew anxious. At first I thought it might be because his twelve-hour workday was taking a toll on him, but the timing was too convenient; it was about a week before Valentine's Day, and my mother told me that men always get weird around Valentine's Day if they are not in a relationship with the woman they're dating.

After two weeks, I'd had enough. I texted him saying that if he wasn't interested in me, he could have at least let me know. Less than a minute later, I received a seven-screen text from him saying that I was a nice girl but that I was right, he had lost interest. I didn't respond. And then I thought: Why *didn't* I correct him? That was when I realized that, as a black woman, silence would never save me. It wouldn't make me more desirable, only more susceptible to whatever a man wanted to give to me, even if it was a pittance.

Before I moved to New York, I imagined the male gaze to be like Doctor T. J. Eckleburg's eyes, which watch over all of Long Island in *The Great Gatsby*. You can never be out of the line of sight. I perused tweets and essays by women whom I admired, in which they proclaimed that they didn't need men to feel beautiful, let alone desired. I envied their confidence. Most of these women were in long-term relationships, whereas I had never been in one of any length and I wasn't quite sure what men wanted. I viewed men as potentially scary, but I still wanted to be desired by them.

After Chris's rejection, I had redirected all my energy into realizing my dream of living in New York City as quickly as possible. Although I moved without a job, I didn't have any college loans, and I saved up thousands while working at a test-prep company for months prior to my move. Now that I was here, I began to think it was normal to live under the male gaze. The first time I walked down the street in central Harlem and I saw a man's head turn as I walked by, I felt an electric current inside of me. I felt human. I realized that I still had a body, that there was more to me than books and literature. So I invested more time in my appearance. I decided to wear MAC Satin lipstick instead of Frost, because its deep purple hue dramatizes my face. I favored wedges over flats so that my five-foot body could be more easily seen. It became normal for me to walk out my front door and have a man call me "beautiful" or "sexy." They were attracted to me, and that attention was addictive. I wasn't attracted to them—but was it okay that I was flattered? Could I admit that I felt like a child tasting something sweet for the first time?

I began to expect these responses—the head swiveling and the compliments—and if I didn't get them, I thought that I was doing something wrong. Being seen as beautiful mitigated the truth that I was in a massive city where few people knew my name, and even fewer cared if I was doing well. The only people with whom I shared substantial conversations were my two roommates. Most days I wouldn't receive a text message from anyone besides my mother. If, just for a moment, I could matter to the gender that I was trying to attract, that momentarily erased my invisibility. But when the moment ended, I'd search for my next fix. It is the conundrum of being doubly subjugated: You are both invisible and hypervisible, stripped of humanity. And if you are not acknowledged at all, even in the most vulgar of ways, then do you still have a body? Are you still a woman without men watching you? Whenever a man asked for my number, I would either give it or lie and say that I was in a relationship. Even now I can never say "no" outright, because I'm afraid of hurting his feelings at best, being attacked at worst. And always—always—I ice my rejection with a smile. My smile is what catches men's eyes the most. I once sat on the uptown 2 train as a group of men discussed how beautiful my smile was; I pretended I didn't hear them.

Because of my smile, a man attempted to woo me in a subway station after we'd made brief conversation about a crazy person yelling obscenities on the other side of the track. He asked me if I had a man, and of course I lied and said yes.

He smirked and replied, "I'm still gonna get you anyhow."

When I learned that he was a native Harlemite, I told him I was unsure how friendly to be to strangers.

"If you don't want to be spoken to, then move to Minnesota or Oregon or somewhere. I don't get why some women have to be a bitch about it," he replied in his strong New York accent.

My smile weakened.

I realized that no amount of smiling or lying to most men can thwart their intentions. If they want me, and there is no other man by my side, then they feel as if they have a right to make advances towards me as soon as I come into their sight. That I don't want them is irrelevant. When men pursue black women, the women are always considered culpable, as if their presence alone is an excuse for a male to act unlawfully. If I am a child on the playground, I am a part of the game to be slapped on the ass; if I am not worthy enough to be assaulted by a black or brown boy, then I am undesirable.

If a black woman in Louisiana did not cover her hair with a scarf, then she could cause a white man to lose restraint. During slavery, the idea of a "Jezebel," or the black woman who has an insatiable libido, was used to justify relations between the slave master and his slaves. This expectation that all we want to do is fuck is reflected in how society does any and everything to suppress and spit on what comes naturally to us, like the hairs that grow out of our scalp, our dance moves, our language. Something must've happened during the first rape of a black female slave by a white captor, when the black man witnessed and could do nothing. She was humiliated, her body splayed open, and we as her descendants have yet to be given our clothes back. Every part of our body is a sex organ. We are present, and therefore we have to be theirs.

WHEN I WAS A HIGH SCHOOL FRESHMAN, THERE WAS A twenty-year-old student who had been held back a couple years, and he always sat at the back of the bus. He would watch me, his eyes circling the circumference of my well-endowed chest before scaling my body. I considered his obvious attraction a compliment, because even more exciting for a teenage girl than captivating a guy is captivating an *older* guy. We exchanged numbers, and during one of our phone conversations my stepfather picked up the phone and was beside himself when he heard a grown man's voice on the line. Before calling me down to the kitchen table, my stepfather called the guy, and as soon as he answered the phone, my stepfather boomed that he should never call the house again or else he would be reported to the police. I don't think the guy got a word in before my stepfather cut him off by hanging up the phone.

When I was summoned downstairs, my mother and stepfather were silent.

"Did you know that that was a grown man on the phone?" my stepfather finally asked.

I shrugged. "He goes to my school."

"Morgan," my stepfather calmly replied, "that was a grown man on the phone. Do you know what he could have done to you?"

And that's when my mother chimed in because engaging in hypotheticals is a strength of hers, a fear tactic that works very well. "He could've kidnapped you, tied you up some-where, and got you addicted to heroin. That's how stuff like that happens." All I did was have a conversation, and my parents thought that was the gateway to a man being unable to control himself around me. For the rest of the conversa-tion, all I could think about was me in a dark basement with disheveled hair and sullen eyes, the guy coming down there regularly to inject me with heroin, and each time finding a vein on my arm with more difficulty. My parents avoided calling me a "fast-tailed girl," but they could have. I was lucky.

Black girls are not just under the surveillance of men, both black and white, but also of their mothers and the elders within their community. The notion of the "fast-tailed girl" reinforces the idea that black girls should privilege the incal-culable eyes on their body rather than focusing on their own conceptions of themselves. Mothers scare black girls into be-lieving that their power is already lost, and that whatever goodness there is in sex and attraction is found only within marriage. If they can scare their black daughters, make them afraid of going back out into the world, then these black mothers will seize some kind of power that they might not have had while they were growing up. When those fearful black daughters become mothers themselves, they will try to reclaim power by instilling the same fear in their daughters. If a black mother can shame a black girl by warning her what she could become, that warning can serve as a vaccine, a small dosage of poison, so that when she goes into another environment, she is already protected. But, of course, it doesn't work that way.

Consent is a language spoken among white feminists in their spaces. This is not to say that Harlem is some lawless place; I believe that it is one of the greatest neighborhoods in the world. And this is not to say that all men do not know boundaries. I have walked past plenty of men who have simply said "God bless you" or "Have a good day, beautiful," and left it at that. But many a woman's "no" may as well be spoken in a different language. Her pulling away from the man may as well as be the opposite because it only builds his excitement and urges him to try harder. If she responds in a way that he likes, she's a woman. If she doesn't, then she's "being a bitch about it," reduced to an animal for not understanding that in this human world of logic and reason, this kind of interaction between men and women is normal.

I HAVE NEVER TALKED TO A BLACK WOMAN ABOUT THE LOSS of her virginity and heard her describe it as anything other than traumatic. There is the undressing, the kisses here and there, maybe a little fondling, and then: an absolute struggle. Some could not even relax their bodies enough for the man to enter them without multiple attempts. In these stories that I've heard, there is barely a mention of adequate foreplay and pleasure is hardly, if ever, discussed. I wonder what is cursing black girls and women with an inability to relax? Are black women also nervous because of how much we have been warned about being "fast-tailed"? Because even if we are in love, we have been taught that lovemaking is not a consummation but a shameful act? If a black girl has grown up fearful of wanting male attention of any kind, how can she release her inhibitions?

I was seventeen years old, and for several weeks straight I'd been having dreams about sex; dreams in which I could count the number of sweat beads on a man's chest, recall our mingling scents, and name any accoutrements in the room. Seconds before waking, my pelvic muscles would spasm and my face would contort. I would wake up with beads of my own sweat decorating my forehead like a diadem and my legs spread. The dreams were so real that I thought that I was in fact being penetrated, that my skin was breaking and something was trying to break through me. After months had gone by, I finally told my mother during a car ride about what was happening in order to make sense of my body. My mother told me that this was an orgasm, but the sensation seemed frightening and not as pleasurable as I'd thought it would be. They left me disoriented, and it took a concentrated effort to refamiliarize myself with my usual surroundings. I was twenty-two when she bought me a small pink vibrator to break the fever, and I kept it in my top drawer hidden underneath loose-leaf paper and jewelry. It looked like an alien; I had no idea how a mechanical object would help.

I pointed the tip at my vulva and winced at the buzzing sensation. After a few minutes, I gave up. I felt embarrassed.

Not too long afterwards, I awoke in the middle of night, *burning*. I was shaking and my heart was racing; I thought that I was on the verge of a panic attack. I thought I would be burned alive from the inside out if I didn't do something quickly. I grabbed the vibrator from my top drawer again, hid underneath the covers, lifted my legs, and rested it on my clitoris. Soon, I was rocking back and forth. I don't know where or how I was able to find a rhythm, but I did and my movements became frenetic, then jerky. Suddenly, my mouth gaped open and my eyelids flickered, my eyes momentarily rolling into the back of my head. I came to splayed across my bed as stars shot across my pitch-black ceiling. And all the while the vibrator, which had fallen out of my right hand, rolled across my blankets, still buzzing.

Around this same time, I remember spending the night at my father's house in Atlantic City, sharing a bedroom with one of my older sisters. She lay sound asleep while I twisted and turned underneath the sheets. Although our twin beds were not the most comfortable, I was acclimated to their feel, and so I knew that my insomnia had to be coming from someplace else. Like I did most nights when I had trouble falling asleep, I peeked through the shutters and stared at the adjacent streetlights and, as I focused, the undulating waves of the inlet. But these tactics were to no avail. My body was on fire. I didn't know whether to strip naked or fill the bathtub with ice to cool down. Yet this heat was different. I was not sweating. My tongue was not dry. I was not out of breath. I did not feel physically exhausted. I thought that I was losing my mind. The only associative feeling I had with this heat was the craving for sex. This craving was so immense that I grabbed my cell phone and texted my mother to tell her that something needed to be done. I was too turned on, and there was not a man in sight who could turn me off by getting me off.

AT FIRST, THE VIBRATOR WAS ENOUGH. I DEVELOPED A NIGHT-time ritual of lifting my legs and moving across the vibrator. And then I found that if I rubbed the vibrator across my clitoris, I didn't need to lift my legs. I moved from underneath my covers to my bedroom floor, pressing my foot up against the side of the bed and sliding up and down against the carpet until I developed rug burn. Initially, my imagination sufficed. I could re-create my dreams, dehydrated and sweaty in a minimalist room; a man who often resembled Bradley would approach me, and there would be a pause between each step, a deliberate hesitation on his part so that he could check my face to make sure I was comfortable with him proceeding. His performance stood in stark juxtaposition to his pursuit, and I would be contorting my body and uttering indecipherable words in a matter of minutes. But as I grew older, and bolder, and more sexually frustrated, I remembered that pornography was only a few remote buttons away. I turned to porn because I was too afraid to have sex with *any* guy after the trauma of repeated heartbreak. Sex, once again, seemed off-limits until marriage. But I could get pleasure without the risks. I'd even go as far as to say that watching porn kept me from compromising my desire to only have sex with someone with whom I felt comfortable; as long as the burning was alleviated, I was fine. I didn't want any man to handle me like the men on my computer screen handled the women. But I did want to come just as hard.

Cinemax and Showtime had the best specials: *The Best Sex Ever, Passion Cove, Hotel Erotica, Nightcap, Kama Sutra.* What if I watched porn while masturbating? It couldn't hurt. The sumptuous visuals and elegant soft-core scenes soon bored me. I wanted messy. Hearing two actors moan, watching their bodies gyrate on each other, was too much of a tease. If two people were going to fuck, then I needed to see *everything*, from the foreplay to the actual insertion. I needed to see the woman's eyes expand as the man entered her for the first time, her hand on his abdomen when she felt like she couldn't take any more, her yell noticeably higher than any of her previous moaning. The ejaculation I could do without.

For me to masturbate in peace to pornography, I first had to get it out of my mind that Jesus was watching me from a dark corner of my room, ready to emerge at the moment of climax. I had to forget that I was still living in my mother's house and she could barge into my room at any moment. I had to ignore the fact that I was terribly lonely and broken by rejection and reimagine myself as some confident, brazen, hot-and-bothered woman. I had to train myself to believe that the actors had known each other for an extended period of time before they had sex; maybe they'd had coffee, or gone to a happy hour together. There had to be some familiarity before they could be so rough with one another. If I had all these pieces, I could be in my zone. I also had to allow myself to accept the immediate shame that came after orgasming from watching two, three, maybe even six people having sex.

Most of the porn clips I enjoyed featured only white

people. White men and women in my mind were like chess pieces, figures that I could move wherever and however I wished, a privilege that I could never have in real life. Watching white women being worn out fueled my most intense orgasms. Especially if the women were blonde. Blonde women in any other context embody the female ideal. Their bright hair and alabaster skin represent their purity. The blonde woman is always the most sought after, the most loved, and the most protected. What better way to destroy her titanic influence on my conceptions of beauty and desire as a black woman than to watch a man splatter cum all over her face? The more painful her moans sounded, the better.

Watching a blonde woman have sex with one man was too gentle a scenario. I relished multiple men pulling on all her limbs, using them to pleasure their penises. I wanted them to take her all at once. I wanted her to be completely overwhelmed, pushed towards the precipice between ecstasy and death. As long as the men didn't turn me off by calling her a bitch or a slut as they rammed inside of her, I was satisfied when they put their hands around her neck or slapped the side of her face. I wanted to hear and see the slaps, the red marks on her body, and the disheveled hair. The more force, the better. I am almost at a loss for words for how consuming these orgasms were. The ripples in my legs expanded to my pelvic region. I would climb and climb as the sensations pushed against me like a strong tide, until the ripples exploded into sparks while I strained to eject that final, strenuous moan. My clit would be so raw and sensitive that I wondered whether I'd burned it off with the vibrator's incessant buzz. I was not at all interested in watching ebony porn. I did not wish to see black women get handled with the same violence. I did not want to see a black woman stuffed in every orifice, even if she was visibly and audibly satisfied by the filling. Each time I saw a penis jammed into her mouth, I wondered if it would block her airways and she would suffocate and none of the men would notice as they continued thrusting. Nothing was fine about watching men—either black or white—pull her panties to the side, jiggle her breasts in their hands, call her "bitch" as if they were calling her "honey." The only times I orgasmed from watching ebony porn was through much effort because I felt *obligated* to do so. Black women were supposed to be sexual beings, wild and carefree. But I was fooling myself. Many of the titles that I came across described a black female porn star not as a "black woman," but rather as an "ebony slut," "ebony hooker," or, the most reductive, "ebony pussy." Although specific language is often part of the fantasy of satisfying primal urges, I could not allow this element to become a part of mine. As a black woman, I felt "ebony slut" or "ebony hooker" made my me-time all too real. I knew that even after I closed that tab, even after that black woman had put on her clothes and walked off the set and into the street, she could still be called an ebony slut. If I saw black people fucking on my screen, I thought about the millions of white people who might be jacking off while watching them and thinking of them not as humans, but as animals or objects. Then again, I was treating the actors in the hundreds of clips I watched in the same vein and with the same disregard.

But the more I watched, the more violent my fantasies became. I transitioned from watching blonde women being doubly penetrated to imagining myself being doubly penetrated as part of some bacchanal in the middle of a tropical rainforest. In a glass enclosure, scientists studied the frequencies of my moans. The men were always those who I knew very well. For a while I was infatuated with a white man ten years my senior, and I envisioned him laying me down underneath a moss-draped cypress tree near one of Louisiana's bayous. It was night, and a strange, thick mist billowed nearby. Apart from the loud crickets in the background, we were alone, kissing underneath a crescent moon. But when I pushed a little deeper into this fantasy—while stimulating my clit, of course—I realized that our clothes were not modern. He wore a long, loose linen shirt, a jerkin, and breeches. I wore a Victorian-style dress and scarf. My God. Was I his concubine? Was I a maid? Was I even free? I tried to back out of the fantasy, but all of these oscillations led me spiraling into one of the most intense orgasms that I've ever had. When I lay back on the pillow afterwards, staring at the ceiling, I was disappointed by what my mind had produced. No matter how hard I tried, I couldn't disassociate sex from social context. There were many other instances where I received the most pleasure from visualizing myself as being unequal to a man: a secretary to a high-powered attorney, a grad student to a professor, a patient to a doctor. I was never his equal. I was never someone he had to address with my rightful name. All of these fantasies ran opposite to my desire that I be loved fully and treated respectfully. But I suppose what made me orgasm revealed the darkest truth about myself: I couldn't see how genuine, healthy love could be associated with sex because sex seemed all about power and I had none of it even without taking my clothes off. At the time, the word "sex" sounded too precious in my mouth. The vowel squeezed between two consonants was too easy to pronounce. It was violent, domineering fucking. I wanted to be crushed.

Black women's bodies are so problematic, so fraught, when it comes to sex. While other parts of black women's bodies, like our hair and butts and breasts, can be seen and slapped or pinched, it's more of an effort for men to find their way to our pussies. When we were enslaved, however, it did not matter if our pussies were closed. Black women's bodies have always been open territory, and our pussies would be opened by force and plundered until rubies were drawn. I wonder if "fast-tailed girl" is the terminology of the intergenerationally traumatized. Our visible bodies may already be sexualized without our consent, but if we can withhold sex or rob a man of the prospect of having sex, then somehow we will be "saved" from being a "fast-tailed girl." But back then, our parents could do little to nothing at all to protect us. There was no withholding of sex. There was no prospect of being "saved" from anything.

But the fact is black girls are sexualized whether or not we withhold sex.

Why can't we be wild? Because we are already wild. Why can't we enjoy sex? Because we are already sexed without clothes ever having been peeled away from our bodies. Why can't we be free? Because we were never free.

IMMEDIATELY AFTER MOVING TO HARLEM, I JOINED TINDER. Kelvin and I went on two dates before he told me that I was looking for a serious commitment that he was not willing to give. There was Etienne, a Malian guy who stood at a staggering six feet, six inches; he tried to woo me with his alleged sexual prowess, but inevitably this scared me off, and I told him that we were better off friends. Leon, a wealthy, suave Nigerian guy who worked in marketing and boasted about his salary, wanted us to spend half of our date in his BMW. When I asked to spend time with him again—since he was attractive and successful—he told me he was busy and never left the door open to schedule anything in the future. All the while, I was writing more online, and this led me to meeting David.

David was a black investment banker with a strong penchant for African-American literature, and he contacted me through a Black Harlem GroupMe message because he wanted to discuss an article I'd recently written about gentrification. Because I had just moved to Harlem, and my friend circle mainly consisted of people from Princeton, I agreed. What I'd thought would be a short meeting at a local café turned into a two-hour-long stroll around the neighborhood, during which we talked about gentrification, blackness, street harassment, and Toni Morrison. I was impressed; I hadn't expected an investment banker to revere—almost worship—Toni Morrison. He was able to quote lines from *Sula* and *Paradise* with ease. Our stroll culminated on my front stoop, where we exchanged numbers. I quickly willed myself to forget about him, trying hard not to fall too fast for a stranger—that is, until he reached out several hours later and hinted that he would love to see me again.

Our first real date took place at a Barnes & Noble on the Upper West Side. He asked me about my dreams and aspirations as we went through the aisles of new fiction and nonfiction. I didn't have to hide any part of myself. Needless to say, I did fall hard for him, and that spiral of desire led to a crash landing. I was a frequent texter and David wasn't, blaming his late responses on personal issues and exhaustion from work. I'd badger my girlfriends asking how to interpret his text messages, and whether his interest was still there. When we were spending time together, he was entirely engaged in the moment. But when we weren't actively spending time together, I thought that I was dating myself. I desperately tried to hold on to our chemistry, waiting anxiously by my cell phone, but I knew he was steadily pulling away from me. We stopped talking altogether when he told me that he did not have it in him to be in a committed relationship. He was stressed out over his job, the prospect of going to law school, and the responsibility of supporting his mother and sister back in Texas. I didn't hear from him for months until I was published on *The New Yorker*'s website and he congratulated me on my achievement.

Believing that, after the long silence, this meant that he was finally ready for me, I woke up at six o'clock on a spring morning to a text from him asking for me to call him as soon as possible. When I did, I soon discovered that he only wanted to be friends with me, although he left the option open for casual sex. I told him that wasn't what I wanted; I yearned for love within a committed relationship.

"You sound like you're falling into the trope of the overachieving black woman who has super high standards," he said.

And I shattered all over again.

Although he later apologized—and I accepted that apology—I felt like a failure on a much larger level than I ever had before. Rejection wasn't because I was too clingy, too outspoken, too aggressive, or too talkative. I was rejected because I was a black woman who was too successful. Somehow all my achievements that I had worked so hard to accrue seemed to be steadily whittling away my dating prospects.

IN THE BEGINNING I THOUGHT THAT MY ANXIETY ABOUT DATing was mine, and mine alone, until I started paying more attention to popular culture and the ways black men fuel this dilemma. Tyler Perry has made millions off of characterizing successful black women as bitter, pretentious, single shrews who need a man to soften their behavior (see *Daddy's Little Girls*), or who insult black men (see Madea in *The Diary of a Mad Black Woman* and *I Can Do Bad All by Myself*, and Angela in *Why Did I Get Married?*). This is not to say that these kinds of black women do not exist, but it is disappointing that Perry, one of the most visible black filmmakers of our generation, perpetuates these stereotypes. What is it about our goals that leads to our stigmatization? Is it because there is a deep-seated fear black women will outpace black men, and the only way to remind us of our place is to withhold love and affection? We may be accepted out *there* in the world with a good-paying job, but that world will never give us love because it wasn't designed to. But when we return to the folds of our community and find that we are denigrated for the skills we used to survive, what else can we do but suppress ourselves just so we'll have somebody?

Coined by Moya Bailey, and further developed by Trudy Hamilton of the now-defunct feminist blog *Gradient Lair*, the word "misogynoir" describes the hatred towards black women specifically manifested through American visual and popular culture. It is so rampant that to try to conceive of ways to eradicate it would be to pull the threads of society apart altogether. Leslie Jones's continual harassment on Twitter for being a black woman in *Ghostbusters* is a prime example. Anytime you see an animalistic or masculine image of Michelle Obama, that's misogynoir. Whenever black women's lives are used as props to empower white women, such as the "phenomenon" of Miley Cyrus twerking or Lily Allen's "satire" in the "Hard Out Here" video, that is misogynoir.

I don't want to believe that David deliberately intended to hurt me, but at the same time he is too smart *not* to know what his statement meant. I wish I could have asked him why he hated me so much before emphasizing to him that, despite what he's been told, I am not his enemy.

It felt like no matter what I did, whether I lived at my mother's house in New Jersey or my apartment in New York, wrote in obscurity or heightened visibility, took initiative or became more submissive, my romantic life always floundered. And because David is black, his comment made me feel like I failed not only on a societal and gendered level, but also on an ethnocultural one, and this failure textured all my past dating experiences. What if I could not keep a man around long enough because I was a black woman who didn't know her place? What if the modifier of being a black woman vacuumed all my other qualities away? It is an insecurity that I am constantly trying to tease out of my consciousness, but that is hard to do when you're reminded of the statistics about black women's marriageability, or lack thereof; every time your grandmother asks yet again if you've met anyone; when people crack jokes about why black women's attitudes are the reason black men flock to white women.

An NYPD sniper tower was set up on Lenox Avenue between 129th and 130th Streets in Harlem, just a short walk away from where I lived during the summer of 2016. I do not know for sure why it was there. It looms in front of the Pioneer supermarket, which is not exactly a hub of illegal activity besides occasional shoplifters whose pictures are posted on the left side of the glass door as you enter. Central Harlem in general is not that crime-heavy. I have walked home at one or two o'clock in the morning, unscathed. I've never been mugged, or heard gunshots. I first thought that because the tower rose around the Fourth of July, maybe the NYPD was preparing for some shit to go down during Independence Day celebrations. But no, that couldn't be it. I moved in around this time last summer, and there had been no sniper tower.

Its tall white presence communicated to all of us that we better not try no shit or *else*. Sometimes a police car would be parked beside the tower, and when one was not, I squinted up to try to see if there was anyone in that tower, but its windows were tinted black. I wanted to ask passersby on the street what was it doing in the neighborhood, but I assumed that anyone's guess would have been as good as mine. I always said to non-Harlemites that if, God forbid, anything happened to me, I would go to the black men who sat on top of upturned crates outside the barbershop or the laundromat before I would ask the police for help. Alton Sterling and Philando Castile had recently been murdered, and their deaths had triggered another cruel summer of black rage that burned hotter than the heat itself.

In late July of 2016, I went to an outdoor jazz concert in Prospect Park. I took the 2/3 train home and got off at my usual 125th Street stop. Usually, if I'm in a good mood or have just finished a significant project, I reward myself with food or drink: a bottle of Perrier, some Talenti gelato, strawberries, kombucha. That evening, I decided I could go for some Mentos before I returned to my apartment and ended the night with a shower and Netflix. There was a deli open at 127th Street and Lenox Avenue, and despite the drug addict lingering around the aisles, hoping that someone could spare her some change, I headed inside. This was the same drug addict whom I'd ignored two blocks earlier by not making eye contact and bobbing my head to the music playing through my earbuds.

As I was entering the store, a man standing to the side of the entrance kept calling me "sweetheart" and attempting to promote a DMX concert. I kept my earbuds in until I approached the counter, as I needed to hear the cashier tell me how much I would have to pay for the Mentos. No sooner did I pay for the Mentos than the man called out to me, and I made eye contact with him before stopping. While he told me about the DMX concert, the drug addict tapped me and held up her right pointer finger. She half smiled, and there were barely any teeth in her mouth. Her hair was disheveled.

I hurried to pull out a dollar because I couldn't stand to look at her any longer; she looked like a figment from one of my nightmares. Once she'd moved on, the man started talking to me about the concert again. Supposedly DMX was having some concert in Harlem and he was in charge of promoting it by passing out flyers. I do not know why he was so aggressive, but nevertheless I felt sucked into continuing the conversation. I asked when the concert was and repeatedly nodded my head, feigning interest in an artist who I thought hadn't been relevant in over a decade.

The man, who introduced himself as Charlie, wanted me to take down his number and call him in order to get tickets at a discounted price. I told him I would memorize it, but he was not satisfied with my suggestion. There was disgust in his raspy voice.

"Nah, see? Why you playin' games? You Harlem girls are suttin' else. You think errbody tryna hit on you and I'm tryna do business. I'm tryna make money. I mean, I'm handsome and all but I ain't tryna hit on you or suttin'. You out here playin' games, you Harlem girls."

"I'm not from Harlem," I said dryly.

What I'd wanted to say in that moment was, *You don't know me.* In retrospect, I think saying that I wasn't from Harlem was a way of evading his overconfidence about having all women in this neighborhood figured out to a science. But in that moment, I was scared. His voice was steadily increasing in volume. Anger punctuated each word he uttered like the strike of an organ chord. The rest of Harlem disintegrated, as if both he and I existed in a vacuum. I felt alone. *What if he hits me?* I thought. *What if he grabs and pins me up against the outside wall of this deli?* So I took out my cell phone and pretended to enter his number in my contacts directory. Luckily for me, he didn't lean over to see what I was doing.

THE WOMAN WHO WENT INTO THAT DELI WAS NOT THE SAME woman who continued home. As soon I walked to the end of the block and waited for the pedestrian light to signal that it was okay for me to proceed, I knew. Something had changed. I had been violated, but I could not name the line that had been crossed. Charlie did not follow me down the block. He did not make lewd remarks about my body. He did not rape me. And yet men, whether posted up beside another deli or en route to a party, now terrified me. The Pioneer supermarket, the soul food restaurants and nail salons, became two-dimensional, as if they could fall down like poker cards.

A police car was parked beside the sniper tower, its red and blue lights flickering. Two male police officers, one white and the other black, leaned up against the side of the car chatting with the ease of the old black men who crowd around the street vendors' tables covered with DVDs and VHS cassettes. The black officer inadvertently glanced at me, and I looked back at him but said nothing. Yet I wanted him to comprehend that my eyes were compensating for my closed mouth; they were yelling for help. But if either of those officers had run to my side and asked what was the matter, I would have gazed at my arms and legs, free of any bruises or marks; looked behind me to see if Charlie had followed, which he had not; and said, *Nothing.* They would have scoffed, thinking I was crazy. And if I *had* found it in me to speak up and say that there was a man harassing women at the deli on 127th and Lenox, then what? This was Harlem, after all. Such things were, for all intents and purposes, normal.

I scurried home. Once I made it to my room, I dropped my purse on the floor and sat at my desk in silence, staring mindlessly at my computer screen. I wanted to grip onto the sides of my desk, fearing that I would lose balance and crash onto the ground. But at least that would have confirmed that I was still on this earth. I was on the verge of tears and I was angry with myself for it. He did not spit at me. He did not call me a bitch or a ho. He did not put his hands on me. He did not rape me. I did not deserve to cry. I had to earn the right to let my tears fall, and when I looked at my unscarred body, I knew that I was unworthy. I repeatedly told myself that it could've been worse and that emotional distress is less significant than physical distress. If I didn't have any scars, then my turmoil should have been something that I could easily get over. It was all internal and should be kept private. I've always been the kind of person who mitigates negative experiences, particularly with men, by telling myself that they were never "that bad."

I texted my male friend with whom I'd gone to the jazz concert; I secretly wanted him to fall in love with me. I told him what happened, and he replied with a sad-face emoji. I was dissatisfied with his response, but what was he supposed to do? Take the subway up to where I lived, which would take two hours at that time of night, so we could go searching for Charlie? And besides, it wasn't like we were dating. So what could I have done? How could I have better defended myself?

My friend is six feet tall and black. If he had been beside me when I went to that deli for those Mentos, I would not have been bothered. I hated myself for yearning for a man to be my shield. And I hated myself for wishing that I had told the police, because they would have tackled Charlie to the ground, and this was Harlem, and we were still black, and I could not have lived with myself had I done that.

White people do not have to reckon with the horror that black people carry in their hearts on a daily basis. I am living in a time when I ache for the son I have yet to conceive. I fear for the day he leaves my arms for the first time to play outside with friends, or to catch a school bus; for any time when he is out of my sight, when I cannot protect him. Whenever he leaves our home, he will be subjected to a law that was never constructed to protect him. Each time I see a black boy or black man, I do not know if that meeting might be our last. Each day that a black person lives is a prayer answered. We mourn continuously with no reprieve.

The summer has never been kind to black people. The Charleston massacre happened in June; George Zimmerman was acquitted of killing Trayvon Martin in July; Michael Brown was murdered in August. And now, that summer, the murders of Alton Sterling and Philando Castile.

I could not have lived with myself if I had reported Charlie to the police because who knows what they would have done? He could have gotten a simple warning, but they could also have tackled him and taken him into custody and done God knows what else. I would subject myself to a black man's harassment a thousand times over rather than watch his face hit the pavement with a police officer's weight on his back. That's not justice. That is a betrayal.

STREETS ARE DEMOCRATIC SPACES—YOU CROSS PATHS WITH homeless people and blue bloods. In most of New York City's streets it is easy to maintain your anonymity if you want. You can choose to ignore a homeless person asking for some spare change. Someone can choose to ignore you if you ask for directions. In Harlem, however, not so much. Black people are communal. If your braids or twists are looking fresh, someone will tell you so. If you are dressed well, someone, either a man or woman, will let you know. On the streets up here there are block parties, psychics offering readings, Cub Scout meetings, voter-recruitment tables, incense vendors, aunties selling sweet potato pies, uncles selling CDs and VHS cassettes, and children selling lemonade and water bottles. Harlem is a constant interaction. You won't see that on the Upper West Side. White people are more protective of their spaces.

The street is also the place where most sexual harassment transpires. Once a woman steps out onto the street, someone can sexually assault her just as easily as someone can try to sell her shea butter. When I first moved to Harlem, it was hard for me to ascertain whether a man was being nice to me because we shared a background and a neighborhood, or because he wanted something from me. One morning while I was waiting on the subway platform, a man walking by told me that one of my earrings had fallen out and dropped onto my chest. I thanked him and assumed that would be the end of it. But as I was putting in my earring again, he stopped walking and told me how beautiful I looked, and asked if he could take me out sometime. I smiled and lied by telling him that I had a boyfriend.

He cocked his head to the left, obscuring the side of his face that presumably bore his disappointment, and said, "Well, he better be treating you right."

In other words, *He better be treating you right or else you gon' be mine.*

Another time I was standing on the train while reading a book and could feel a man's presence hovering over me.

I looked up, and a guy said in a long, drawn-out manner, "Your height is sexy. How tall are you?"

When I told him, he boasted that he was six feet, five inches and then asked if he could take me out on a date.

"I got a boyfriend."

"How long y'all been together?"

"Eight months." I should've said eight years.

"Eight months? That's it?"

"It's very serious, trust me."

That wasn't enough, for he proceeded to offer me money to go out with him. At the next stop, more people flooded the subway car and so I moved to the middle and found a seat where I could read in peace.

IN OCTOBER OF 2014, AS TWENTY-FOUR-YEAR-OLD SHOSHANA Roberts walked around various New York City neighborhoods in jeans and a black crewneck shirt, she was catcalled and harassed by 108 men. The experience was recorded by *Hollaback!*, a photoblog and grassroots initiative to raise awareness about street harassment. The video went viral, and by 2016 it was reported that the less-than-two-minute video had received 40 million views on YouTube.

This video sparked many discussions, but the one that most struck my attention was that the majority of the men who catcalled Shoshana were black and Latino. Although I am not sure what Shoshana's racial background is, she physically presents as white, and I am concerned with how easy it is to paint men of color as ruthless aggressors against an innocent white woman. Some of the instances in which a black man told her to have a nice day or called her beautiful did not seem like harassment to me. Sure, their intentions were probably underscored by their attraction to her, but is that harassment?

I watched that video while I still lived in New Jersey and so I kept all these questions to myself. But now that I live in Harlem, I question if the black men here would have relentlessly catcalled a woman who looked like Shoshana. I'm sure that white women do get harassed in Harlem, but not with the same amount of vigor and aggression as black women. Because unlike white women, black women exist outside the law. Historically, if a black man so much as whistled at a white woman, he could be lynched. If a black man whistled at a black woman, that was chivalry. If I had gone to the police on the night that Charlie harassed me, would they have thought that I was overreacting, or worse, would they not have believed me? Because I was not physically harmed, would they have told me that I was being oversensitive because Charlie was most likely just being nice?

In 2014, Feminista Jones, a blogger, author, and creator of the #YouOKSis campaign, told an *Atlantic* reporter that despite the positive intent of initiatives to stop street harassment, such as Stop Street Harassment (SSH), these movements still place white women at the center of their advocacy. The police are not exactly our allies either. They can abuse and rape us with impunity. It is a strange position that black women occupy, and it results in a difficult question: How do we protect ourselves if that means chastising black men, whom we have always been culturally conditioned to protect? What does this dual protection look like, and is it attainable in a society that sanctions violence against black bodies?

When I think about how Harlem's streets are a place of conversation, economy, and community, I start to second-guess myself. Maybe the only goods that Charlie was trying to sell *were* tickets to a DMX concert. Maybe what he wanted was only money, not to climb on top of me. Maybe I misjudged his calling me "sweetheart" as patronizing when he really was just trying to be nice because he did not know my name. Maybe I was being conceited. Maybe I cried because I was still getting used to the city environment, not because I thought he was going to hurt me. The more excuses I made for him, the less trusting I became of my body and my own instincts.

And that sniper tower. It is still there. I do not acknowledge it now when I walk by. I keep my head low and my headphones nestled against my ears. I walk in a fashion similar to that of all the other black women with whom I cross paths every night as I return to my apartment. I wonder what kind of secrets they are holding in their bodies, what kind of experiences they have buried to protect someone else at their own expense. Whom they could run to for help.

As I write this, I've just passed my one-year anniversary of living in New York. I have only been on two dates in the past eight months, out of circumstance and choice. Fear encapsulates both of these experiences. My heart palpitated at the thought of what these men could do to me, how they could tremendously hurt me, paralyze me, even though all they did was ask what drink I wanted, or if I was having a good time. Both situations ended with the guy not being interested, and making this clear either through silence or long text messages. Each time, I thought back to my college years and wondered if there was something inherently wrong with me. I wondered if I was *too much* of everything, leaving no room for a man to find his place beside me. I wondered if my desperation reeked so badly that the stench made men stay far away from me. I wondered if, with each byline that I snagged, I was becoming less and less of a woman, unlovable just as David had said. I wondered if writing this essay would be the last nail in the proverbial coffin of my romantic life.

I haven't heard "fast-tailed girl" spoken as much as I have before, but that could be because I don't hang out around any black female teenagers. But that doesn't make me worry less for them, wherever they are. I am still concerned about myself, a grown woman who desires to be a wife and mother. I am concerned about the women who are already mothers, the mothers in progress, the daughters, and the daughters who have yet to be born.

But I have not given up hope yet. I am learning to love myself. I took a solo vacation, satiated by my own presence. I came back to Harlem feeling refreshed, ready to transform my energy so that I could take the risk of falling in love. But that deep-seated fear still lingers in the pit of my chest, even if it does not pulsate as it did before. I am trying to shed the fear that maybe I am diseased as a black woman, chalking up these experiences to growing pains on the road to true love. I just wish that these pains didn't hurt so badly.

5

A LOTUS FOR MICHELLE

Dear Michelle,

In July 2008, approximately six months before your husband assumed office, *The New Yorker* published a cartoon by Barry Blitt that featured the both of you as terrorists. The theme was "The Politics of Fear," and it was the front cover image. Barack is in Muslim clothing and you are in military garb and have an AK-47 strapped to your back. You are fist-bumping in what seems to be the Oval Office while the American flag burns in the fireplace. Many called the image offensive and disgusting, but nevertheless the magazine's editor, David Remnick, deemed it satirical, for it held up a mirror to the stereotypes swirling around about Barack's faith. But for me, the more problematic issue was how you were portrayed. Unlike Barack Obama, whose

seemingly smooth hair was underneath a taqiyah, your hair
was transformed from your usual permed shoulder-length
hair to a large afro—the cartoonist accentuated the countless coils. They resembled barbed wire. Your lips are pursed,
almost identical to the kind of gesture that many black
women make when they are perturbed or in the midst of
saying something witty. Your eyebrows are raised and your
head is cocked to the side. Your lips, unlike Barack's, are
colored red, perhaps to accentuate their fullness. Your eyes,
unlike Barack's, are open and spilling over with intent. The
AK-47 strapped to your back is the least terroristic element
of this image. Contrary to popular belief, you, not Barack,
are its true focal point. You are the one whose body is
most exaggerated. You do not incite terrorism with bone-
straight hair and good posture. No, your body is forced
to reflect what America must imagine in order to strip
away your exceptionalism: a large afro, gestures normally
ascribed to the sassy black woman stereotype, and a gun
for good measure. If this image was supposed to satirize
"Politics of Fear" surrounding you and your family, then
it succeeded because that image was exactly how many
in white America could only see you, Michelle: through
double vision. They rejected what their actual eyes perceived: an extremely accomplished woman whose career
many of them would have been lucky to emulate. Instead
they replaced you with an aggressive and violent woman. As
long as their imagination is entertained, their belief in their
inherent superiority as white people could be sustained.

I was too young to really engage with this image. I was
only sixteen years old and I wasn't raised in a particularly

political home. I did know, however, that we were Dem-
ocrats and that in my community, the Easter bunny was
more believable than a black Republican. I had heard of
the possibility of a potential black president but only within
the realms of comedy, such as Eddie Murphy's *Delirious*,
Dave Chappelle's "Black Bush" skit on his Comedy Central show, and Richard Pryor's "Black President" skit on
his show back in 1977. It seemed like only through black
comedy could I, and many others, consume the idea of a
black president. Perhaps this was the only space where we
could delight ourselves with the idea, through laughter,
because if we seriously considered it, we would have worried that he would be assassinated as soon as he was sworn
into office. But when you, Barack, and your daughters,
Malia and Sasha, walked across the stage after it became
official that he would become president, I went into my
mother's bedroom where my stepfather, Z, was peacefully
lying on his side of the bed. He smiled at me, but we did
not say a word to each other because something in our cores
was shifting and we needed time to ourselves in the midst
of being close to each other. I will be honest and say that I
do not remember President Obama's full speech, but what
I can vividly recount is the single tear that fell down my
left cheek. It was the first time I had cried from someone's
oration, but it was more than that. I had an actual image
of black ascendancy. It was not a two-dimensional portrait, a subject of a comedy skit, or an idea casually thrown
around among ourselves, but a physical reality. But I did
not dream of becoming president like Barack. You were
the one who enraptured me. Barack's voice was merely the

background noise to the relationship that I, and millions of black women around the world, would have with you.

Your story reads almost like a myth. Your great-great-grandfather Jim Robinson, the first documented member of your family tree, was born on Friendfield Plantation in Georgetown, South Carolina, which is over 450 miles away from the White House. Slaves lived in tiny white-washed slacks that lined the dirt road en route to this rice plantation, and it was there that Jim, after emancipation, worked as a sharecropper, toiling in the rice fields along the Sampit River, and lived with his wife, Louiser, and their children. We don't know how Jim died, but local historians believe that his body is located in an unmarked grave that commands a view of old rice fields on the outer limits of White Creek.[6] Robinson, his wife, and his children comprised the last illiterate branch; each descending branch of the family was more educated than its predecessor.

Born on the South Side of Chicago, you showed your intellect quite early on, skipping second grade before entering a gifted program in sixth grade. After graduating as salutatorian from your magnet high school, you went on to Princeton University, a place where your teachers told you that you would never be accepted. I know what that's like, too. My white female guidance counselor suggested that I go to community college when I was in the top 5 percent of my class and assumed that my parents weren't wealthy enough to afford a place like Princeton. When you read your acceptance letter, did you grip the edges of the paper out of fear that it would disappear? Did you cry?

When you were making your way to campus, were you

afraid? Back in 1981, Princeton was considered the most conservative of the Ivies; it still is. But I know, beyond a shadow of a doubt, that your experiences with racism were more overt. Your classmates asked to touch your hair like you were an object that could be crushed down to the small size they needed you to be in order to make themselves feel great. When the mother of your freshman roommate, Catherine Donnelly, discovered that you were black, she called her alumni friends to object, even going so far as to visit the student housing office to get Catherine's room changed. Her grandmother begged Catherine's mother to take her out of school entirely. Catherine Donnelly's grandmother wanted Catherine out of the school immediately and to be brought home. How did you feel then? Did you ever walk down Prospect Avenue—"The Street," as we call it—and marvel at the eating clubs, some of them eerily similar to plantation houses? If you dared to walk down The Street, were you afraid that some drunk white jock or the son of some finance tycoon or a scion of some political dynasty would yell "nigger" as you passed or throw things at you? Where did you find your place of refuge during your four years there, and how can many other black women, who are still fighting for recognition and respect, find theirs?

You do not know the impact that you had on the black female student body during my time at Princeton, even while we waited with bated breath for you to return to campus, to no avail. It felt cruel that you would not at least stop by and talk to us. But our complaints tapered off when we more deeply considered just how much unnecessary affliction you endured as an undergraduate. This story of your suffering at Princeton is yours and yours alone, but if we could have known more of it, perhaps we would have felt less alone. Still, we forgot that you aren't just our First Lady, but the whole country's, and that perhaps you simply didn't have the time. We wanted a piece of you to ourselves because whether or not we could articulate it then, we know now that some of the ways in which we see are only possible because of our shared identity as black women. We wanted to hold on to that preciousness for dear life.

I entered Princeton in 2010, exactly twenty-five years after you graduated, and your ascendance sparked an almost cult-like following among black female students; you provided hope as we obsessed over black male desire. We outnumbered the black men three to one; it was a sort of bloodbath. Statistics told us that our professional success would imperil our chances of ever getting married, and we were quite aware how much the odds were against us at Princeton. There were very few black women who were successful in finding relationships. The perpetually single ones like me overanalyzed this incessantly rather than chalking it up to luck, God's favor, or anything in between.

Tell me, did you have these same anxieties while you were at Princeton? Did you date anyone and worry that your dreams alongside the simple fact of you being a black woman made you an unsuitable partner for anyone, black or not? Did you question your worth?

At least, during my time there, my classmates and I were fortunate to have you, an example of a black woman who excelled and fell in love with someone who did nothing to diminish her. Your story was referenced so many times that your importance became biblical, deserving of a book or chapter of its own somewhere after the book of Ruth and before Proverbs 31. You were never "easy." At Harvard Law, you dated Stanley Stocker-Edwards, the son of Patti LaBelle, and you later said, "My family swore I would never find a man that would put up with me," as though you were a nuisance rather than a blessing standing beside a lover. What was it about your personality that anyone would have to put with? What does it say about your family that they thought that the life you sought to live would be met with a scoff from a man? In those moments, did those comments bounce off you like Teflon or stick like molasses?

In the introduction of your senior thesis, "Princeton-Educated Blacks and the Black Community," you wrote, "My experiences at Princeton have made me far more aware of my 'Blackness' than ever before. I have found that at Princeton no matter how liberal and open-minded some of my White professors and classmates try to be toward me, I sometimes feel like a visitor on campus; as if I really don't belong . . . These experiences have made it apparent to me that the path I have chosen to follow by attending Princeton will likely lead to my further integration and/or assimilation into a White cultural and social structure that will only allow me to remain on the periphery of society; never becoming a full participant." This might have been the case when you were at Princeton and later at Sidley & Austin, but what about as our nation's First Lady? What happens to white people's eyes when you eschew the periphery, when you become the most visible woman in the world? When they turn on the television,

they see you meeting with heads of state from all over the
world. When they flip through magazines, there you are
smiling and wearing the finest of fabrics created by de-
signers who seek to put the best of their wares on your
statuesque black figure. When they close their eyes and
think about this country's direction, blackness is carved and
curved into two figures: you and Barack. That is inescapable. It is the kind of upheaval that black people have
patiently waited for white people to experience, even if
your eight years in front of us are not enough to overturn
centuries of oppression. But I pray that they at least briefly
knew what it meant to feel like the "other" whenever
they saw your smile and the elegance of your stride and
that it scared them. Damn, those eight years felt good.

Do not think that they have not tried to grapple with
their inner turmoil, a kind that was collective across the
world. Before writing you this letter, I researched images
of racist photos of you, and I swore not to look at them
the night before I began writing out of fear that I would
not sleep. Once I woke up the following morning, I realized that I had made the right decision. There is an image
of you dressed in a red gown with your back exposed,
your face beautifully made up, your wrists bound and tied
together with a thick rope presumably hanging from a
tree. The Ku Klux Klan is in the backdrop. Another image is from a Spanish magazine called *Fuera de Serie*. It's
your face superimposed on an African Guadeloupean slave
painted by the French artist Marie-Guillemine Benoist in
1800 and one of her breasts is exposed. This is what they
need: to create images of you as an object en route to a

cruel, racist death. But hey, at least you look beautiful.
At least you have on a red gown or a beautiful headscarf
while you're on your way to being cast out of this world.

You were the only First Lady to have two Ivy League
degrees, you tied with Eleanor Roosevelt for tallest,
and, of course, you were black. You were not the kind
of blackness that could make white people feel at ease.
You are not light-skinned with gray or green eyes, and
your hair is not curly. Unlike Barack, you cannot claim
a white parent and in turn white people cannot claim
any stake in your success. You did not get pregnant
out of wedlock. There are no images of you smoking
weed or any other substance. You do not have a crimi-
nal record. It is a shame that you had to be this spotless,
that you had to be, in every sense of the word, perfect.

Because no one could find any flaw in you, they made
you feel worthless just by being in your body. Photogra-
phers shot and dispersed images of you with your mouth
open while in the midst of a conversation to "show" that
you were animalistic. Cartoonists exaggerated your five-
foot-eleven frame by adding extra muscle in your arms
and bones in and around your cheekbones to make you
appear more masculine and Neanderthal. Snapshots of
you with your lips pursed were circulated to make you
seem like the typical sassy black woman with an attitude. Fuck the Ivy League degrees, the high-powered
attorney position, the many accolades to your name.
You were still black. And even worse, you were a black
woman, and they would never allow you to forget that.

What did you do to take care of yourself during all

this humiliation? Did you pour love into your family, and did they reciprocate? Did you read the works of Toni Morrison, Nikki Giovanni, and Toni Cade Bambara to realize that you were never alone? Did you listen to Nina Simone as you applied a pomade to your skin and hair before going to bed? What did you do to remind yourself that you are brilliant and accomplished despite the efforts they made to belittle and squish you into a narrow prism so that they could live peacefully? What did you do?

On the night of the 2016 Republican National Convention, when Melania Trump plagiarized your speech word for word, were you flattered, disappointed, or fully expecting something like that to happen? A white woman snatching the words from a black woman's lips and defended by some on top of that. That's not newsworthy; that's history, how it's always been. I was reminded of a time in high school when I wrote a speech from which a white female classmate read because she was a part of student council and I was not. I stood next to her on the podium during graduation, silent as she read. When Melania recited your speech, where were you? After living in the public eye for over eight years, perhaps you have created a mental armor with a thickness that this offense could not penetrate.

Then again, I'm very certain that you have grown even stronger, for during Hillary Clinton's presidential campaign, you spoke with the kind of confidence and vigor that drew tears from the eyes of millions of Americans. Ninety-four percent of black women who voted in the 2016 election voted for Hillary Clinton. Ninety-four percent—many of whom probably had family members who were affected by the 1994 crime bill that triggered massive incarceration rates, particularly among African-Americans. This bill expanded the death penalty, obliterated federal funding for inmate education, and motivated states to lengthen prison sentences. While speaking in support of this bill, Clinton called African-American teenagers "superpredators," and while she apologized for this statement, she still said it. And yet black women rolled up their sleeves and voted for her while white women—53 percent to be exact—decided that a racist, xenophobic, misogynistic man with neither government nor military experience deserved to be president. Now, ain't that some shit? Hillary Clinton, the patron saint of white feminism, couldn't depend on them on Election Day, despite all the celebrity support and pantsuit flash mobs. Of course, the immediate response to the rise of Donald Trump is that everyone was to blame for his victory, but the numbers say differently. When white people attempt to generalize blame, it is a tactic that further enables white supremacy, for the rhetoric obscures those who should really be held accountable: white people themselves.

On Tuesday, November 8, 2016, white people chose white supremacy. They chose to ignore how Trump incited white nationalists and called for surveillance programs directed towards Muslims that were reminiscent of those from Nazi Germany. They chose to ignore the many women who accused Trump of sexual assault. They chose to ignore Trump gloating over doing so. Why? For one, most of his terrifying plans do not affect them. They can turn down their lips and bow their heads in pity, but they will never be targets. They wanted to make Amer-

ica great again by turning the hands on the clock back-
wards; they wanted everyone to know their place; they
rendered the racial and social hierarchies of our country
even more calcified. In essence, on Election Day, they
chose themselves because historically they always have.

And as for the white women who voted for Trump,
I suppose that they left their vaginas at home before they
went to the booths. Again, these white women believed
that their proximity to white men would allow them to
partake in white male privilege. These white women
chose their race without taking into account the implications of gender. In fact, there were some white women
who showed up to Trump rallies with shirts that stated
that they would love for Trump to grab them by the
pussy. Somehow, under this man, under his fascism, they
felt protected—even honored. This is a true feat of mental calisthenics. But then again, I've never had the privilege of believing that my racial identity can smooth over
or compensate for the oppression associated with being a
woman. That's the thing about whiteness: it's blinding.

Immediately after Trump became president-elect,
there was a push for you to run in 2020, but I'm not sure
that America deserves you. I cannot imagine the number of psychological and political battles you fought while
in the White House as First Lady, but you mustn't forget how much we black women loved you. You were not
afraid to dance on live television, shoot hoops with LeBron
James, rap, and appear at black-women-centered events
to remind us that you were still an active participant in
our world no matter how injected you were in theirs.

Michelle, when you said that you live in a house that was built by slaves, something must have crystallized for millions of Americans—the proof is in how many white people tried to discredit your statement. You might have been destined to work in the White House but not to sleep, eat, and host there. The White House was never meant to be your home.

Everything does in fact come around full circle. The great-great-granddaughter of an illiterate South Carolinian slave whose body rests in an unmarked grave near rice fields was the First Lady of the United States of America. You are not Eleanor Roosevelt or Jackie Kennedy. You are Michelle Obama, the embodiment of a new dream that is characterized by both role reversal and intergenerational revenge. We do not need to be subjected to the lie that is the American Dream. You are the beacon that reminds black women that they can be anything they want to be in this country. You are the beacon that reminds white people that 99 percent of them will never reach where you are: their whiteness cannot carry them there; your achievements lie far beyond their grasp. You are the beacon that reminds us that the ascendance of a black woman like yourself is possible, and what a blessing it was to see you shine. You are not an animal or a man. You may be a terror. But their terror is our delight.

For you, Michelle.

6

BLACK GIRL MAGIC

I AM ONE MONTH SHY OF TURNING SIXTEEN WHEN MY STEPFA-ther is diagnosed with degenerative frontotemporal lobe dementia. He is fifty-eight years old, a former lieutenant colonel who received medals for his service in Desert Storm, and a tenured psychology professor who regularly visits local mental hospitals and takes calls from suicidal patients in the middle of the night. One dinnertime, he regaled me with the story of how Lord Byron's challenge to Mary Wollstonecraft Shelley to write a ghostly tale led to the creation of *Frankenstein*. I smiled and nodded my head as I swirled my green beans around on my fork, but I didn't believe him. He is just a psychologist, after all. How could he pull out random literary anecdotes with such ease? Before him, I never saw a black man harness such a talent. Later that evening, I found out via Google that he was right. After that, I never question his knowledge again. Instead, I drop my eating utensils and rest my chin on my right palm while he entertains me with Shakespearean recitations or hypotheses about Napoleon Bonaparte's rise to power. I have to remember these memories when he becomes unable to string coherent words together.

HOW DOES IT BEGIN? I AM NOT SURE. ONE DAY AS I PULL MY curtains back to let the natural light into my room, a habit that he encourages me to develop as a tactic to ward off depression, I notice that when he gets out of his car, he falls on the ground. This, at first, doesn't alarm me. He is six feet, six inches tall. That's a whole lot of human. He gets off the ground, dusts the grass blades off his backside, and starts towards our front door, but the quiver in my heart ripples throughout my body with more intensity when I watch him forget the groceries sitting on the same patch of grass where he'd fallen. I am afraid to ask my mother what is going on, because I am afraid of what she might tell me. And then he begins to forget the groceries at the supermarket, returning home with only the long receipt in his hand, bewildered because his arms are not carrying anything. He paces around the house in the evening, checking, double-checking, triple-checking, quadruple-checking, quintuple-checking all the locks in the house and the knobs on the stove. When he, my mother, and I go to a wedding expo to prepare for my sister Patricia's impending nuptials, he is unable to figure out which utensils to pick up, and the names of certain hors d'oeuvres.

Small giggles underscore his questions, but by now I know something dark is happening. He is embarrassed, but nevertheless I help him make his plate. We do not speak for the entire ride home. My mother follows me into my bedroom and closes the door behind her. It is gray outside, and the drizzle soon starts. She tells me the truth.

By my sophomore year of college, he has already surpassed the doctor's initial prognosis of two years. But I cannot think about that right now. I am busy establishing a rapport with my roommate, Denise; I have early-declared as a comparative literature major; I am working on a novel and also cowriting a play for a struggling black-centered arts company. I am not thinking about him—at least, I think I'm not. I am present, but a part of me is vanishing.

MY STEPFATHER, MY MOTHER, AND I ARE HAVING DINNER AT home and I smell something strange coming from upstairs. I smelled it before, but I assumed that it was coming from outside. Now, it intensifies, and I casually walk up the steps to see a full laundry basket next to a night-light, and smoke rising to the ceiling. I yell and immediately grab the basket, dragging it down the steps as fast as I can. By this time, the blankets in the basket are on fire, but luckily, my mother has a large towel to smother the flames. All the while, my stepfather stands there as though he is simply watching a bonfire, waiting for the heat to be just right so that we all can make s'mores. He has a cup of water in his hand and he flings it onto the blankets, but by then the fire is out. He is too late. He is far too late. What if I hadn't been there? What if this had happened while my stepfather and my mother were asleep and I was back at college? What if the house caught on fire and my mother couldn't escape because she couldn't convince him that there was an actual fire? What if I had received a call while I was in the middle of my eleven a.m. Japanese class, the police telling me that their bodies were charred beyond recognition? What then?

I don't sleep that night. Something on the inside of me is breaking, splintering in slow motion into innumerable shards. I thank God profusely for making sure I caught the basket in time, but unconsciously something in me shifts. I have to pace around the house, stand in front of the back-yard windows and squint to see if any figures are moving around outside, turn and twist the stove knobs multiple times to make sure that the burners are really off; I have to hear the flicker, see the blue flame flare and disappear, and *don't you move until you do this at least four or five times.* I check all the night-lights to make sure nothing is near them, not even a dangling phone cord. I turn on the alarm when I leave, but the confirmation beep does nothing to make me move away from the keypad because I have to stay there for several minutes to convince myself that it is actually working, despite the red light indicating that the house is armed. My heart races whenever I walk past an open drawer revealing knives and forks. I am not suicidal. I want to live. But what if, in a split second, I harm myself? What if I drag a knife down my arm, poke at the skin underneath my eye with a fork, press a burning skillet against my thigh? What if?

I don't trust myself anymore. Many nights I wake up with both ears ringing, my throat tightening, and my heart sprinting. I don't know if it is a panic attack or just my new life. It happens to be both: a series of panics. Every night, I set my alarm for seven a.m., but I click it on and off more times than I can count. It does not matter if I see the alarm icon in the upper right-hand corner of my cell phone screen. Did I see it? Did I see it? Did I really see it? If someone were to put a gun to my head and ask me, *Are you sure?*, could I have said beyond a shadow of a doubt that I was?

I go to two sessions with an on-campus psychologist, but I am afraid of going to her for more because if she finds out that I am losing it, I might be urged to take a year off from school. She categorizes me as having mild OCD. She suggests outside psychologists, cognitive behavioral therapy, maybe even medication. I do not explore any of these options. Black people do not *do* therapy. Although my stepfather is a psychologist, he is an outlier in my environment.

Why should we employ modern science when its advancements would not have happened if black bodies weren't being exploited? J. Marion Sims, the father of modern gynecology, experimented on enslaved black women without their consent and, in his autobiography, praised three slaves' endurance to withstand experiments without any anesthesia because their contributions would help all women. Doctors at Johns Hopkins took the cells of Henrietta Lacks and used her genetic material for medical breakthroughs for over six decades without her permission. Benjamin Rush, the father of modern psychiatry and cofounder of the first anti-slavery society in America, believed that all black people, or "negroes," suffered from negritude, or blackness. Rush argued that blackness was a mild form of leprosy that could only be cured by becoming white. He also asserted that Africans went insane due to slavery. If this is our legacy and we cannot trust the systems in place, where else can we look but up?

We go to God with our problems. Therapy is for white people with money. It is a pastime, a hobby, a luxury. It is for the religiously and spiritually lazy, not for us. How dare I admit my weakness when my people have survived far worse than a sick stepfather? Black women had to take care of everyone: their masters, their husbands, their mistresses, the mistresses' children. I thought being able to withstand any and everything was not only my responsibility but also a gift from my foremothers. The Strong Black Woman is the backbone of her family, home, and community, and so she is supposed to be a bit aggressive. She is able to withstand any kind of pressure or pain. She doesn't need to rely on anyone but herself. She does not hurt. On the surface, this ideal is a compliment to black women's resilience and endurance, but it dehumanizes us by not acknowledging our human weaknesses and needs. The Strong Black Woman does not ask for help not because she does not need it. Her emotions are crushed underneath that totem. She is always willing, always giving, and easily taken advantage of. Because what other option is there? What avenues does she have through which change can be a possibility?

WE HAVE RECLAIMED THAT RESILIENCE AND TRANSFORMED IT into self-empowerment and self-love in the form of "Black Girl Magic," both a phrase and a movement. Black Girl Magic is, according to writer Clover Hope, "a declaration of pride amongst black girls and women." However, its singular definition is as elusive as the person or company who claims the term.[7] The long-held belief is that CaShawn Thompson, a feminist writer, popularized the international phenomenon in order to "counteract the negativity" of the images of black women in our society. It began as a Twitter hashtag and grew into a movement showcasing the accomplishments of black women like Beyoncé; actress Amandla Stenberg; writer, producer, and director Ava DuVernay; Olympic gymnasts Simone Biles and Gabby Douglas; the Williams sisters; and former First Lady Michelle Obama.

But in 2016, Elle.com published a controversial op-ed by Dr. Linda Chavers, a scholar of twentieth-century American and African-American literature with a PhD from Harvard, about Black Girl Magic. When she heard the phrase "Black Girl Magic," Dr. Chavers interpreted it as synonymous with the Strong Black Woman stereotype. She argued that glorifying black women during their highest moments obscures their suffering, which is another form of dehumanization. In a subsequent interview with *For Harriet*, she admitted that she did not know much about the movement, but went on to explain that "if we keep perpetuating suggestions of being exceptional, we're getting into dangerous territory. We've done it before. We've done it again, whether we originate it or it originates explicitly from white supremacy, to me, it doesn't matter." She also reinforced that she loves black women and apologized for not making that explicitly clear in her exploration of the issue.

When Dr. Chavers's article went live, it was met with immediate backlash from black women, including myself. I was thrown that an academic would not do her research on a movement before writing about it; the move seemed to undermine her training as a writer and scholar. Others could not understand why such a piece was published on a mainstream, predominantly white website, and felt like it was an editorial failure for it to have been green-lit in the first place. In fact, some even suspected that it was a conspiracy on the part of the editors to make a black woman a puppet; her article dismissing an empowering movement would get many hits while she would be left to the wolves. About a day later, a rebuttal by writer and editor Ashley Ford appeared on the same website, arguing that Black Girl Magic is not about being superhuman but rather reclaiming what others refuse to see in us; it was much better received. But as I sat longer with Dr. Chavers's piece, I felt less spite towards her and more remorse about the way her point of view was almost immediately dismissed throughout social media networks, especially Twitter. Although I agree more with Ford's argument, I regret that there was not a larger discussion about what it means to be a part of Black Girl Magic. Dr. Chavers said that she did not know much about "Black Girl Magic," but who can honestly claim that they do? There are many ways to counteract negativity. And what the backlash only scantily acknowledged was that Dr. Chavers is disabled.

Four months after her Black Girl Magic piece, she published another essay on the same website describing her battle with multiple sclerosis. She opens by talking about how her hand suddenly begins to shake uncontrollably while she's giving a lecture on Albert Camus's *The Plague*, and so she worries that her students will think that she's nervous. About the intersection of her blackness, womanhood, and disability, she writes, "Chronic illness is, if nothing else, an education in how much every single part of your body actually matters. As a black woman, it doesn't take much to make me hyper-aware of my body."

The vast majority of the images, individuals, and accomplishments showcased by the Black Girl Magic movement are of able-bodied black women. Gymnasts who can tumble and fly through the air as though natural law bends to their will, and not vice versa. Actresses who express themselves with great fluidity throughout a range of scenes. Politicians whose words, ringing clear like a bell, can have the impact of a tidal wave. Musicians who can sing, play, and move with great versatility. Activists whose bodies are at the front lines of nationwide protests and pepper-sprayed, handcuffed, and sent to jail, only to rejoin as soon as they are released. While these black women may not be as heralded as their white female counterparts, they are overwhelmingly more prominent and praised than black women with disabilities. Physically disabled black women are virtually invisible in our cultural landscape. We do not usually see them making music onstage, as love interests in movies, or as emblematic black beauties in fashion campaigns. They do not become Barbies, congresswomen, award-winning scientists. We have no Amy Purdy or Marlee Matlin or Jacqueline du Pré or Jamie Brewer. According to the US Bureau of Labor Statistics, in 2014, black women ages sixteen and up had the highest participation in the labor force at 59.2 percent. White women trailed behind at 56.2 percent. However, that same year, 22.2 percent of black women with disabilities participated in the labor force, almost seven points behind the participation rate of white women with disabilities at 29 percent. Black disabled women also have the lowest income out of any other race/gender disability category.[8]

Still, tracing the black female body politic from slavery to present day, we think of how our vaginas were raped by white slave masters, how our stomachs became swollen with children who were sent out in the fields as soon as they could walk, how our backs were rent and blood would gush from our torn flesh, how our breasts were drained by white children. How our hair is seen as wild and animal-like, our asses as emblematic of our inherently grotesque nature, our skin color the basis of all white people's problems with us, and our womanhood an extra incentive for them to invest their hatred in us. We are constantly remembering how our bodies were never our own, and movements like Black Girl Magic are reclamatory because they demonstrate what we can achieve with our bodies when we have autonomy over them. But for black women with disabilities, autonomy is a battle fought both from without and within. Every morning, I can rise from my bed, make myself breakfast, take a shower, do my hair, and dress. None of these tasks is a struggle. But for a physically disabled black woman, just getting out of bed in the morning—an ability I take for granted—may require a herculean effort. She must wrestle with her own body before she can expend any energy on how the outside world perceives it and the space it occupies there.

BLACK WOMEN FACE A DIZZYING CONUNDRUM. WE RESIDE outside the margins of a white patriarchal society and thus we are often dehumanized. To regain our humanity, we focus on what it means to be a black woman, where black women can find safe spaces, and how black women can protect ourselves within white spaces. These are worthy concerns, but they assume a black woman's physical body is still perceived within our own community as "normal." As Crystal R. Emery said in her 2016 essay for *Time*, because she is a black woman with a disability, a "wheelchair-riding quadriplegic," she is stigmatized in three ways: for not being white, male, or able-bodied. The dismissal of Dr. Chavers's words reinforces our ableist privilege. Her second piece should have prompted us to recontextualize her original argument, but unfortunately it received less than 126 Facebook shares; her first essay received over 9,000. We do not teach young black women that they should recognize and aspire to the achievements of black women with disabilities, perhaps because we know so little about them—and we must change that.

I USED TO CALL IT MY "SECOND TONGUE." MY LEFT INNER labium protruded approximately four centimeters from my body, and I do not remember it ever looking different. It was thick, wrinkly, and long, and I thought the extra skin was fun as a child, a bigger appendage that I could play with. When I pulled back the flap of my left labium majora, my left labium minora would immediately unfurl like a tongue. My mother would frequently pop into my bedroom when I was changing for church or gathering my towel to go into the bathroom to bathe and ask, "That thing doesn't hurt?" With my legs together, I would look down at myself, my vulva seemingly neat from that vantage point, and shake my head. That "thing" did not hurt, until it did.

The pain began somewhere around middle or high school. If I wore stockings underneath my plaid skirts or dress pants, the nylon would rub up against my inner thighs and the friction would cause my vulva to protrude and my "second tongue" would unfurl again, sometimes even sticking out of my panties. When this would happen, I could only readjust the elastic band and hope that that this would push my left labium minora back into its original, hidden position. Wearing shorts was its own kind of torture. Denim chafed against it, pain surging and swelling from the inside out. I figured that if I began a strict exercise regimen I would lose weight in my thighs and that would eliminate the chafing altogether. Unfortunately, I soon realized after several weeks of elliptical and treadmill sessions and calorie cutting that most of the weight I lost was from my stomach and face. No dietary regimen could stop my "second tongue" from growing.

When I moved into an apartment in Harlem that had no air-conditioning, the humid ninety-degree weather presented another challenge. It didn't matter if I wore stockings, shorts, a tight skirt, or a maxi dress: my left labium minora would still stick to the inside of my panties. I would trudge the two flights of stairs to my bedroom, close the door behind me, place my two fans on the opposite sides of my desk chair and turn them on to the highest intensity, sit at that desk chair, remove everything from the waist down—my left labium minora hitting the seat before any other part of my body—and delicately massage in whipped shea butter until the pain subsided. I never thought that this ritual was problematic because I never assumed that this pain was a problem. I never assumed that it was a problem because I assumed that pain was an integral element of womanhood.

I GOT MY FIRST PERIOD WHEN I WAS TEN YEARS OLD, AND the first several times I was plagued by severe migraines. When I whimpered and complained to my mother about never wanting a period again, before giving me a Midol she told me that I would have to deal with this for decades. When I had my first gynecological exam, seconds before the speculum was placed inside of me, I looked at my mother sitting to the right of the table and she said, "This is just a part of being a woman," believing that that solidarity would help. It didn't. When the speculum opened me up, my face contorted as I tightened every muscle in my body because I believed that the gynecologist had gone too far, that I was too open. I wanted to be closed again. I learned from my mother that pain from first-time sex and birth was normal, even to be expected. My conceptions of pain were inextricable from my conditioning as a cisgender woman, and the pain I experienced from my "second tongue," along with the meticulous rituals to soothe it, made me feel not only womanly but also superhuman for being able to endure it. I thought that the pain in and of itself was in fact admirable. I was able to present myself to the world as a bubbly, eloquent, and educated black woman while the site of my womanhood afflicted me. I thought: *This is how I will become strong, through how well I can obscure pain.* I was never taught that the world would nurture me, so I perfected the ways of hiding. I figured that because I was born with a longer labium, I was destined to take care of it. If I relinquished that honor, then I would be unworthy of this life that I have, this grand body that I inhabit. I did research to support my theory. Women of the Bahima clan, in western and southern Uganda, keep their labia minora long enough to cover their vaginal opening in order to make access harder for potential rapists. In Rwanda, girls will pull on their labia for ten to twenty minutes a day in order to lengthen them so that once they marry, their husbands will have an easier time making them orgasm and squirt. Some women, particularly those in Zimbabwe, have even gone as far as getting procedures in order to *stretch* and *elongate* their labia. *See?* I thought. There were other women of the diaspora who had, or aspired to have, long inner lips just like mine. Maybe, I thought, it was some kind of badge of honor, even though the only marks I received were the extra ridges appearing along its surface from years and years of chafing and sticking. The more I focused on it as a gift, the more I was in denial over my own personal body. I trained myself to normalize the pain until I shamed myself whenever I sensed its reemergence, but in the recesses of my mind I wondered if all of this endurance was necessary. When I became a more active feminist during college, my desire to grit and bear the weight of my left labium minora intensified. Publications such as *Mic*, *Broadly*, and *Cosmopolitan* emphasized that labiaplasty stems from insecurity; those who underwent the procedure were victims of the pressure from the patriarchal society in which we all live, where women are expected to be perfect. One of my closest friends in college was a premed major, and she tried to dissuade me from labiaplasty, suggesting documentaries about the misogyny surrounding labiaplasty procedures. I didn't have the heart to tell, or show, her the size of my left labium minora so that she could better gauge my situation.

If I underwent the surgery, would that make me less of a feminist? And if I became less of a feminist, what standard would my feminism be measured against: white women's?

My doubts didn't stop me from scheduling a consultation with a fancy Long Island doctor in late 2014. My mother and I drove to his plush office, where I had to remove everything from the waist down and lie back on an examination table while the doctor used what looked like a Popsicle stick to poke my labia to show my mother and the nurse where incisions could be made to make me symmetrical. I felt like I wasn't in the room as a whole person. No one made eye contact with me even though one of the most vulnerable parts of my body was being scrutinized. After I dressed, my mother and I were directed into the doctor's office, where he showed us before and after photos of past patients, before going off topic, chatting at length about his views on terrorism and his son's active service overseas. I was stunned. I mean, this was my *vagina* that we were talking about, a vagina that had yet to be penetrated or give birth to a child. A vagina that, for lack of a better word, had not been used. My vagina was wholly private, wholly mine, which made me feel all the more vulnerable about this process. The doctor's assistant, his blonde and well-groomed wife, assured us that everything would be fine before giving me a student discount for good measure.

It took me over a year, and much discussion with my mother, to decide whether I would go through with the surgery. The same thoughts kept swirling in my head: Was I a bad feminist if I went through with the surgery? What if the only reason I wanted it was because I was worried about what some man would think? What if the pain was all psychological, a direct result of my insecurity dealing with the body that God gave me? Why couldn't I just deal with the pain? I wasn't suffering from some chronic illness. I didn't have cancer. I didn't have gangrene or hepatitis B. Why couldn't I suck it up? The pain was not impairing my life at all. My foremothers had gone through far worse, and I had the nerve to care about some extra skin between my legs. *That's not strength*, I thought, *that's cowardice*. Then I remembered all the times I'd had to skillfully maneuver the lower half of my body while in the midst of conversation so that no one would think that there was something wrong with me. I thought about frequent bathroom trips and the subsequent pain whenever I tried to readjust. I relived the thick of summer when I was both hot and sore, when time would pass me by as I sat with my legs splayed across the floor. I didn't tell anyone other than the man who I was starting to date about my imminent surgery.

I did not have a chance to be afraid. For the entire duration of the car ride from my Harlem apartment to Long Island, I tried to memorize my body's topography: every blonde hair on my arms, dry spot on my face, stretch mark on my thigh, gnawed skin on the sides of my fingers. I chose not to have my procedure in a hospital because I wanted as short a recovery as possible. In the weeks leading up to the surgery I'd had to get a handful of shots; fill a series of pre-scriptions for hydrocortisone cream, Vicodin, and Percocet; read through an informational packet about what I must do pre- and postoperation; and take a call with the doctor so he could elaborate on any part of the process. The packet seemed like a fair list of rules and guidelines, such as no eating before the operation and mandating that I shave my vulva before I went into the office. One page listed what might happen to me: nerve damage, sexual dysfunction, scarring, death. I swallowed a large wad of saliva as I read, figuring that this was standard practice as well. I'd had a root canal years ago, when I also could have theoretically died. The last page, however, was what almost caused me to renege on my decision altogether: it was titled "Psychological Healing." *Psychological healing?* I was reducing the size of my inner left labium, not getting a hysterectomy or a mastectomy. What kind of psychological healing did I need after a surgery that would last no longer than an hour? Although I couldn't get this out of my head, I never spoke to the doctor about it.

As I sat in the waiting room, the receptionist instructed me to take one Vicodin and one Percocet. Afterwards I was escorted into an exam room, where I took off everything from the waist down and stood up against the wall adjacent to the door. The doctor crouched down in front of me while the female nurse stood watch in the near corner, perhaps to thwart sexual harassment accusations. He asked me to part my legs and then he pulled down my inner left labium in order to photograph its original length. I focused on the fluorescent lighting overhead, my eyes spasmodically blinking in concordance with each camera snap. I felt humiliated.

But once I lay down on the exam table, I didn't feel that way anymore. Inside, I was pulling away from my core, like dandelion seeds being stripped away from the flower by the wind. The doctor injected the local anesthesia into my vulva and praised me for being able to hold still. Truth be told, it was easy; I was not in my body.

As the doctor cut away, my mind drifted. I thought of food and documentaries I wanted to watch on Netflix. There was not a moment where I thought, *Hey, pay attention to what's going on.* I felt like I was levitating. Even when he grabbed the forceps I did not flinch. I saw part of myself wedged in between his right pointer finger and thumb, the same digits I used to adjust it. When he placed what he'd taken from me on a draped table, I wanted to twist my neck to look at it, but my head was too heavy to move.

After I was stitched back together, he showed me how much he'd cut off. That part of my "second tongue" was about as wide as my two thumbs pressed together, its consistency similar to that of an elephant's skin. My mother came into the room and helped me to put back on my clothes and stand up. We stopped for lunch at Chipotle on our way home.

In March of 2016, I was allowed to attend the Association of Writers & Writing Programs (AWP) conference in Los Angeles. AWP is a prestigious three-day extravaganza teeming with agents, editors, MFA students, creative writing instructors, publicists, readers, and, of course, writers. There are an overwhelming number of panels and parties, occasioned by an industry fair that features over 850 exhibitors. I was only several months into my job as an editorial assistant, one that I had dreamed of getting for over a year, and I had stars in my eyes the whole time.

One night, an acquaintance invited me to a party at the Silver Lake home of the writer of some Oscar-winning film. Because the friend of said acquaintance offered to drive us and one of my mentors would be there as well, I decided to go. We walked into the backyard, and the party was exactly how I'd envisioned it. Hordes of mostly white people, including a few authors whom I recognized because of their recent releases, bobbing their heads and casually sipping on vodka next to a pool. I decided to stay sober. There wasn't a chaser to help with the vodka, and these were not my people. I had to remain professional.

Kristina, a young Latina from New York whom I'd met at a Halloween party the year before, was swimming in the pool along with several other guests. She spotted me and swam over to the side, urging me to come in, too. I smiled and politely declined. I was only one of perhaps four black women there, and I didn't need to stand out any more than I already did. I wanted to explain my decision by saying I didn't want to mess up my hair, but I didn't think Kristina would understand this; although she was a woman of color, she could easily have passed as white because she was very fair-skinned and had blonde hair. I'm sure she had on many occasions. My second option was to say I didn't have a bathing suit, but before I could speak, a black woman got out of the pool and told me that there were communal bathing suits in the house. (I wanted to give this woman the side-eye for even *suggesting* this. Growing up, I learned that black people's personal hygiene standards were different than those of white people. We cannot refuse to wash for days, or not wash our hands after using the bathroom; poor hygiene is a privilege reserved for white people, who can eschew certain modes of decency and still be considered clean. Why would I want to put my body in a bathing suit that I couldn't be sure had been thoroughly washed, or washed at all, since it was last used?) I sat down on an adjacent sofa, but that didn't stop Kristina from trying a second time, and then a third, to get me into the pool. I could not tell Kristina the truth, that I was uncomfortable and afraid, because I worried that she would think that I had some kind of social anxiety disorder.

Then again, maybe I do.

Now that the other woman had left, there was no other black person in that pool. Some of the people in there were smoking. Men and women were making out with one another. There was a weird vibe, like the pool activities could have easily progressed further. For a moment, I felt like an extra on the set of some *Entourage* episode; these were the kinds of behaviors that I only saw in decadent HBO series, or read about in personal essays written by white women. To me, such hedonism was a luxury afforded to the white and privileged, and when I was in that world I could observe but never participate. At the most I could afford a glass or two of the weakest wine, but I could never indulge. White, privileged people are always considered clean no matter what they do, while I as a black woman have to constantly scrub at the filth that society smears onto my body.

I feared that if I got into the pool half naked, with my breasts spilling out of a bikini top, my body would alter the atmosphere. I would be stared at, and men might even hit on me, asking me where I was from and if I was having a good time before offering me drugs. If I got in and didn't participate with everyone else, I would be seen as uncool and immature. If I did, someone I knew professionally could see me, suspect that I was up to no good, and then my boss could find out that his most recent hire was fucking up.

When I discussed this deep sense of unease with my mentor, who is also black and more than ten years my senior, he told me that I made the right decision by not swimming. He eased my worry that I was overthinking an otherwise fun situation. In fact, he argued that there is no limit to over-thinking when you are a young black woman in an over-whelmingly white space.

But a part of me *wanted* to fuck up. I *wanted* to see what it was like to be so carefree, so white. I fantasized about get-ting in that pool, taking off my bikini top, catching the eye of some older and more powerful editor, and having sex in a bathroom with the door slightly cracked. I thought about what it would be like to do a line of cocaine, even though I've never wanted to. (I have a strong aversion to taking even regular, over-the-counter drugs.) But these fantasies were the only luxury in which I could indulge. Only in my imag-ination could I do any of these things and remain unscathed both professionally and socially.

I crept back into my hotel room that night so that I would not disturb my roommate. I couldn't fall asleep, so I decided to read and propped open Melissa Broder's essay collection, *So Sad Today*. Broder is the creator of the depressing, anxiety-ridden, and self-deprecating Twitter account @SoSadToday, which has over 370,000 followers (including Katy Perry and Miley Cyrus the last time I checked). Plenty of my friends retweet her posts. I don't, but I do read them whenever they appear on my timeline, usually half smiling at their relatability before diverting my attention to something else that won't pull me into such a dark place. For years, Melissa's identity as the mind behind @SoSadToday was hidden. She published poetry under her real name in many renowned magazines and journals, like *Guernica* and the *Missouri Review*. When I googled an image of her, I saw a blonde-haired woman with smoldering eyes, simultaneously inaccessible and vulnerable. Reading her biography, I assumed that she was a woman who had her shit together. She was so accomplished.

Generally, I devour personal essay collections written by women in a matter of days. I'm a nosy and voyeuristic person, maybe because I have four older sisters and I know what it feels like to be banished from their conversations. I listened from the outside and vicariously lived through them. Or maybe I'm naturally curious. Whatever the reason, I love reading about women's inner lives, traveling through the pages like a boat buoyed by a mild yet noticeable current. But reading *So Sad Today* was like trudging through a stalactite cave. It felt dangerous, as if I were violating Broder in some way by reading the secrets that she shared and gave permission to publish. She spent pages upon pages writing about how much she destroyed her body in her early twenties with whiskey, benzodiazepines, opiates, Ecstasy, laxatives, amphetamines, psychedelics. I sank into her accounts of blacking out all over San Francisco, waking up to blood on the walls and strange men next to her in bed who told her how much of a mess she was, going into yoga class with the alcohol oozing out of her pores, the whole time feeling more and more guilty for enjoying these darkest moments of her life. All the while I thought, *How the hell is this woman still alive?* Even more, *How is she still alive and so successful after all that?*

Then again, I already knew how her story would end: she would not only still be alive; she would be writing and producing and traveling and talking and gaining visibility. She would rise from the ashes of the fire she'd started, like the phoenix of Greek mythology. Soon, it became clear to me why I chose not to swim in the pool that night: because as a black woman, I was never taught that I possessed that kind of regenerative power.

OUR CULTURE LOVES YOUNG, BEAUTIFUL, AND DRUG-addicted white women. In the mid-1990s, heroin chic was all the craze in the fashion world. Characterized by the dark circles around their eyes, gaunt bodies, pale skin, and either drained or apathetic expressions, supermodels like Kate Moss and Jaime King rose to prominence. Of course, this trend was criticized by anti-drug groups and even former president Bill Clinton, but its timing was not an accident. Because of the scars from the 1980s crack epidemic and the fear of AIDS, heroin was seen as a "healthier" alternative due to its relative purity, and its use was glamorized not only in fashion but also in the music world. Aside from the reality that the fashion industry (like most industries) is overwhelmingly white, I am not surprised that white models popularized "heroin chic." Growing up black, I was imbued with extreme hatred for Ronald Reagan and his administration; I knew nothing else of his impact on America besides the crack epidemic. Little black girls were traded by their parents for twenty-dollar rock; prostitution skyrocketed; an entire generation of low-weight "crack babies" was born to addicted mothers. Because of Reagan's War on Drugs, by the end of 1999 over half a million black men and women were sitting in state and federal prisons, broadening the disparities in incarceration rates between blacks and whites.[9]

As a child, I never saw black female television characters experimenting with drugs or alcohol—only their brothers. Sure, they might have had fake IDs, multiple boyfriends, and an occasional disregard for their parents' rules, but that was it. Yvette Henderson of *Smart Guy* is a straitlaced teenager who has a passion for women's rights and eventually attends Georgetown. In one episode, her younger brother, T. J., gets drunk one night. Moesha is a witty—and often boy-crazy—teenager from Los Angeles. When her brother stores a marijuana cigarette in his room, their parents initially accuse Moesha, which catalyzes a discussion about drugs. The creators of both shows, Danny Kallis for *Smart Guy* and Ralph Farquhar, Sara V. Finney, and Vida Spears for *Moesha*, chose to keep both black female teenage characters spot-clean. The same goes for Tia Landry and Tamera Campbell of *Sister, Sister*, and Reagan Gomez's character, Zaria, on *The Parent 'Hood*.

On the contrary, drug and alcohol use and abuse seems to

have been a rite of passage of white female characters of the 1990s and 2000s. Rayanne Graff, of *My So-Called Life*, gets addicted to both alcohol and drugs and suffers an accidental overdose that leads to her having her stomach pumped—yet she is also a fashion icon because of her layered outfits and accessorized hair. In *Degrassi: The Next Generation*, Ashley Kerwin takes Ecstasy, Anya MacPherson develops a cocaine addiction (but quits on her own to join the Canadian Forces), Katie Matlin abuses OxyContin and goes to rehab, and Victoria Coyne takes crystal meth. On the other hand, Hazel Aden, one of the most prominent black female characters, never so much as lifts a bottle of vodka for the five seasons where she appears. Kelly Taylor, of *Beverly Hills 90210*, gets addicted to cocaine thanks to her boyfriend Colin. Andie McPhee, of *Dawson's Creek*, gets accepted to Harvard and experiments with Ecstasy pills. The list goes on and on.

What all this taught me as a child was that drug and alcohol use was an "oopsy" mistake for the vast majority of middle- and upper-class white girls, who might indulge if they got bored on a Saturday night. Even if they did experiment with drugs for a little while, white girls would still go on to great colleges; they would marry well and have children, regaling their teenagers with stories of their past. Wash, rinse, and repeat. That's not to say that white girls and women do not succumb to drug addiction. They do many times over. But as a black girl, if I so much as *touched* a pill there was no coming back. There is no space for "experimentation" in the world of young black women, for there are already too many obstacles to overcome. Unlike with white girls, our inherent innocence is not assumed. We don't have the space to be reckless and carefree and then "healed," regenerating and then returning to regular life. Blame is already draped upon us like a cloak, but not one that can be shed at will.

When I see my white female contemporaries post pictures of their asses, or facetiously call each other sluts, or share their exploits on weed, LSD, or Klonopin on social media, I know that if I did the same I would embody a historically entrenched belief that I, as a black woman, am nothing but an immoral and filthy animal at my core. I knew this quite well at that Silver Lake party. As a black woman, I knew I could not afford to make a mistake. Fulfilling the expectations of society's white imagination would be to self-inflict an injury from which I could not recover.

ONCE MY MOTHER AND I HAD RETURNED TO OUR FAMILY home after my surgery—she was not comfortable bringing me back to Harlem, where no one would be looking out for me—I felt that I was dirty and that I needed to take a shower. The anesthesia was wearing off, and so she gave me another Vicodin and another Percocet. Almost as soon as I'd swallowed both pills and stepped into the shower, the soapsuds barely beginning to form on my body, I told her that I needed to get out because I was going to slip and fall. I crash-landed into her king-size bed. Bleeding and blabbering characterized the next forty-eight hours, which passed in an opiate haze. I felt as if someone had unplugged me. Fuses were blown out throughout my entire body. I was never vertical for longer than a few minutes, and I barely spoke because I did not have the ability to do so. As soon as the pills traveled down my throat, I began to slip away. I couldn't feel a thing, and I hated it. I wanted to feel the pain because it was mine, mine to bear. I was afraid that I might get hooked on the pain meds. I was terrified of the desire to disconnect from reality, the root of much drug abuse—and *that* was really the last thing I wanted. I had fought so hard to both survive and thrive, and I didn't want anything to soften or eradicate the intensity of life altogether. After two days, I swore off the Vicodin and Percocet. I wanted to feel the stitches in my body. I wanted to have some kind of sensation to remind myself that I did go through with a labiaplasty procedure, and that I was alive. So I opted for Advil, which was enough.

After the extended weekend was over, my mother begged me to take the rest of the week off work to recuperate, but I adamantly refused. I was still working at my hard-won entry-level job in publishing, and although I'd informed my (male) boss that I was having a procedure, I didn't go into details; I wasn't about to stay home for a week and refuse to provide a full explanation. I had to prove myself not only because I was new, but also because I was a black woman in an industry where minorities make up less than 5 percent of the workforce. I dreamed of success, and that started with me being strong and pushing through whatever pain I had. I'd chosen to get this procedure and I had chosen to deal with the consequences. I'd be damned if I presented as weak in front of my coworkers. As a black woman, I knew I had to be twice as good, stitched vulva and all.

Her name was Irie Thomas, and she was an older cousin of one of my former best friends. Six years my senior, she had grown up with her grandmother in an apartment that my real estate agent mother had sold to them. Like many teenagers, she was rebellious, and I never had much to say to her when I was young, partially because I was afraid of her. Her most striking trait was her eyes: intense, dark brown, able to focus without blinking.

By the time I was applying for college, she'd had a child and was starting to frequent my Pentecostal church, initially sitting in the farthest pew and only socializing with a very few people. But her eyes were friendlier, with a more consistent smile balanced between them. She was glad to see me and I her. She wanted to know if I had talked to Ruby lately, and I wanted to know how she was able to squeeze a healthy baby out of her petite body. We exchanged numbers and began to talk regularly.

Despite being a student at one of the worst high schools in South Jersey, I was confident about my college chances. I was in the top 5 percent of my class, I had taken several advanced placement courses, and I had received a competitive score on the SATs. I was extremely private about where I was applying, even with my parents. I had it all planned out. On April 1, I would get my acceptance to an Ivy League school—or to a couple—and drive down to my father's house with a cake in the passenger seat, iced with the names of the schools where I had been accepted. I wouldn't even call him. I'd just surprise him, and then afterwards he, my mother, and I would all get dinner and then stroll along the Atlantic City boardwalk in a celebration of my new life's trajectory. But it did not happen that way. Emerson College: Accepted. *Duh, of course. That was my* backup *school.* University of Miami: Accepted, with an academic scholarship. *Duh, of course. That was my other backup school.* New York University: Rejected. *Wait, what? It wasn't exactly a backup, but then not necessarily a reach. It's okay. I didn't want to be in a place with no campus, anyway.* Yale: Rejected. *Okay, I guess. I loved the campus, but there are still more.* Columbia: Rejected. *Columbia, too? I . . . Okay. Okay, I* guess. Harvard: Waitlist. *No. If you are just going to reject me, reject me.* By the time Princeton let me know I was on the waitlist, I was completely gutted and in a catatonic state. Tears fell from my eyes, but I could not feel them rolling down my cheeks. My sadness paralyzed me. My mother tried encouraging me, and then she pulled out the phone cord from the jack so I wouldn't get calls that I didn't want to answer. She had all sorts of suggestions about how I could run away from the disappointment of this day. My father eventually called her cell phone, wondering why he could not reach the house, and my mother told him what was going on. He wanted to speak to me, but I refused. I could hardly speak to anyone. It's not that Emerson and Miami weren't good schools—they were great schools. I could've studied writing with the best teachers at Emerson. The University of Miami gave me a merit scholarship, which was going to alleviate the financial burden since my then-sick stepfather, our family's breadwinner, had stopped working and my mother was his caretaker. But I just thought for sure that I'd get into at least one Ivy League school.

The following week, I discovered that a fellow classmate and friend had been accepted to Harvard, his dream school. Our beloved English teacher, Mrs. C, threw him a party after school at which I mostly remained silent while picking at my pretzels and cheese puffs. My friends understood how sad I was. One of them told me to be patient, that it wasn't technically over, but that year Harvard had over 700 names on the waitlist; Princeton, 1,400. I had been sending letters with updates of my accomplishments to the Harvard admissions team; Princeton did not even encourage this kind of follow-up, so I painfully stayed silent. There was no way that I would get into either of them unless a miracle happened.

ONCE IRIE HEARD THE NEWS, WE BEGAN TO SPEAK EVERY night, and she would listen to me talking (or, more accurately, blubbering through my tears). Her concluding prayers were always long and intricate, and as she prayed I could feel my chest expanding, my breathing becoming less labored. She prayed for peace, discernment, strength, and, above all, God's will to be done. I hated the last part. What if God didn't want what I wanted? But towards the end of a month of consistent prayer and communion, while deep under my covers one night, I prayed for strength, and for God's will to be done. The words poured out of me like water. I surrendered because I discovered that I had no other choice. That was when He met me where I was.

Soon afterwards, Irie called me up and said, "You are going to hear something on Wednesday at noon. Do you receive it?"

In disbelief, I answered, "What do you mean?"

She repeated her question again, this time with more urgency. I agreed, and then she hung up.

I grew up recognizing the power of women in my church. Pentecostalism is a "charismatic renewal" movement within Christianity that emphasizes a direct and personal relationship with God, and although men might have occupied more positions as preachers and reverends, women's spiritual talents were more evident. For years, I had watched women prophesy to other women, men, the homeless, and drug addicts after peering down at them from the pulpit. I had seen women place their hands on people's heads and watched those people, who were sometimes two or three times the size of those women, fall on the ground, speaking in tongues—a sacred language that is believed to be only comprehended by God—and waving their hands around before an usher covered them with a white cloth. Men, women, children, and infants would clamor to reach the front of the church, many crying, many shaking, a few falling over, all with their eyes closed. Speakers would also move in and out of the crowd, pinpoint someone, move towards that person, and prophesy to him or her. We called these women who had the gift of healing and prophesy, whether through touch, prayer, or anointing olive oil before giving it to someone in need, "prayer warriors." Sometimes prayer warriors would form circles with other women whenever they needed God to make a move in a given situation. Other times, they would claim vivid dreams that foretold the future.

My grandmother Sylvana was a prayer warrior. Every morning, she would seclude herself in her closet and pray for all her loved ones. Plenty of times she would dream about fortune or misfortune portrayed through symbols, such as vines and birds. I wasn't quite sure that Irie was a prophetess. She seemed too young, and she wasn't trained in biblical doctrine. But her unwavering voice forced me to believe with all my might that something was coming to me on Wednesday at noon.

A few days passed, during which I was starting to warm up to the idea of attending the University of Miami. I liked Miami, loved it actually. I loved the palm trees and the beaches, and the carefree attitude that Miamians all seemed to have. I thought I could get used to an ibis as my school's mascot. I even imagined myself holding up my hands like wings out of pride for my alma mater. And then I received a voice mail. I assumed that it was from my mother, telling me to take out the trash before I did anything else—she always left me messages like this—but I listened to it anyway. It wasn't from her. It was from a woman at Princeton, who indicated that she had called me at noon. It was Wednesday.

Once I got home to my bedroom, I took a deep breath and called her back. I thought that I would have to go through an interview of some sort, some final fiery hoop to prove that I could do the work there, but when she answered the phone, she didn't waste any time in telling me that I was accepted and that she would send an acceptance letter in a few days. I hung up the phone and started crying. When I called my mother, she screamed. Immediately, my house was infused with a fresh burst of happiness.

That same night, my mother drove me down to the church to give my testimony. I gave the testimony again at the following Sunday service, and Irie sat in the back, silently crying with her hands clasped near her face. I don't know whether the congregation was captivated more by my story, or by the realization that the quiet single mother in the last pew was a prophetess. In retrospect, I realized that I needed that month in a holding pattern to really wait and see what God could do. Getting off Princeton's waitlist demonstrated more of His glory because it seemed the most impossible outcome. Fourteen hundred names. *Fourteen hundred names.* There is no amount of math or science that can rationalize what had transpired. Irie had predicted the exact date and time that something great would happen to me, and it did. And this would not be the only time that Irie's prophesies came true. During my commencement weekend, Irie texted me the words "bidding war" in relation to my writing dreams. She knew no publishing lingo, and only asked that I receive her message. Two years later, I did get into the midst of a bidding war; my proposal sold at auction, which is how this book came to be.

ENCHANTMENT, MAGIC, AND FAITH-BASED POWER HAVE ALways been a pervasive force in African-American life. For slaves, accessing the supernatural was a way in which to undermine white domination and possess power in day-to-day conflicts. In his memoir, Frederick Douglass writes of a conjure man named Sandy Jenkins, a fellow slave who provides him with a root that will protect him if and when he finds himself in a confrontation with a "negro-breaker," or slave disciplinarian. The black abolitionist and writer Henry Clay Bruce, who had been enslaved in Virginia, discovered a community of slaves who sought the help of a conjurer in order to thwart deportation and removal to a plantation in the Deep South, where conditions were presumably more brutal. At the last minute, their relocation was cancelled.[10] Slaves moved from conjure to Christianity with little to no concern about the supposed incompatibility of these two belief systems.[11] Slaves' encounters with Christianity were deeply fraught—some had it foisted upon them, and others were actively barred from it. Indeed, white supremacy has been inextricably linked to Christianity in America. Some slave masters took up the task of converting their slaves so that they would remain obedient at all times. Many believed it was God's will for Africans to be enslaved so that they would be brought closer to Christ. But masters tended to hate it when slaves actually made Christianity their own. Slaves were forbidden to have prayer meetings, so they met secretly in wood and ravines, among other places. Some masters forbid their slaves to go to church because they believed that they didn't have souls. Despite all these adversities, including not being able to read the Bible for themselves, slaves crafted sermons, songs, and dances blended with ancestral African traditions and their present-day experiences.

The rise of Pentecostalism in the 1800s saw ritual healing and protection, as well as the notion of supernatural help, become more closely aligned with traditional Christian practice. Because black people in the United States lacked sufficient medical care, even after emancipation—if they were treated, it was often with contempt by white physicians—they turned to herbalists and conjurers for healing. Both Pentecostal prayer warriors and conjure specialists believed that the spiritual and natural worlds collided in their practice; they each relied on supernatural, invisible powers to restore the wholeness of an afflicted client, even today. For the former, God is the vehicle through which these miracles spring forth, whereas for the latter the source is more ambiguous. Some conjure specialists believe that their talents are divine, and others say that their powers derive from objects and charms that they have created.

DANIELLE AYOKA IS A FORMER PRAYER WARRIOR WHO NOW describes herself as a clairvoyant, astrologer, and magic maker. I found her on Twitter because so many religious and spiritual black women who I follow regularly retweeted her advice and admonitions. She says that when she prayed at night as a child for negative thoughts to leave her mind so that she wouldn't have nightmares, they would go out of her bedroom window and she would watch them slide away like a movie reel. She became a prayer warrior while at Norfolk State University, through her participation in a campus youth ministry. Like the women in my church, she would lay her hands on people, mostly black children, and they would cry, fall on the ground, or both. To strengthen her spiritual gifts, Ayoka would fast for five to seven days with only water for sustenance. She would read and study different religious texts for hours, abstain from sex and alcohol, and shy away from parties. In college, she began to study quantum physics and energy, which made her feel as if her needs were not being met by the kind of Christianity in which she was raised. She met a woman named Mya, who became her spiritual adviser. On All Saints' Day, an important pagan holiday, Mya dreamed that a crow was pecking at Danielle's forehead; she explained that crows represent consciousness in Native American religions. During Ayoka's first healing session, when Mya instructed her to lie down, she all of a sudden felt her lymph nodes close up. When she told Mya she couldn't breathe, Mya snapped and wiggled her fingers, and told Ayoka that she'd had a terminal illness in her past life that needed to be cleared up. Once Ayoka left the session, she felt lighter and happier and subsequently invested in energy sessions monthly. Not too long afterwards, she learned from her father that she comes from a lineage of Native American shamans. Now, she practices quantum healing, which involves manipulating energy in her clients' bodies in order to shift it.

Ayoka rejects the idea that black women are particularly vulnerable to shouldering more than our fair share of burdens in our society. In an interview, she says to me that we do have "a strength and endurance, and [that] is unmatched.

"It has been passed down from generations," she adds. "It is what we've seen from our mothers, grandmothers, and great-grandmothers. The way in which we go through life—we are able to be a support for everyone. When is the last time that you've seen a black woman break after everything she's been through and she wasn't able to get through that? You don't know another black woman who has been through some things? We have been there for others. We have been strong. We have raised each other's children. We have helped each other to survive. No one can take your power unless you give it."

When I spoke to another black woman, a witch named Haylin Belay, about why she practices, her thoughts were eerily similar.

"The deepest forms of magic in the United States come from Native Americans and black people," she said. "I get a lot of empowerment out of my witchcraft. I wouldn't feel that empowerment anyplace else . . . There has been multiple times that I've shouted in 2016, black women have a lot of problems. We are being gaslit every day, and we have to deal with trauma, abuse, and harassment. I have to go through this world questioning if people see me as a full human being. Despite how others may treat me, I have this core, this form of resilience. My magic is where no one outside of me can touch that . . ."

I have difficulty accepting these women's ideologies because they seem to be validating the Strong Black Woman stereotype. But then I wonder if spiritual strength can override any obligation black women feel they have to fulfill on earth. Perhaps if our strength resides outside the physical world, a world that is largely influenced by a white supremacist system, then our being Strong Black Women is not a stereotype, but rather an honor to uphold.

As my sophomore year progresses, my stepfather deteriorates and so do I, but I still can't bring myself to go back to the campus psychologist. Growing up in my black Pentecostal church in South Jersey, I was told that Jesus was the answer for everything. God is supposed to be my solid rock and fortress whenever I face trials and tribulations. My faith in God is absolute; I trust He has the answers for everything. Suffering is a huge component of Christianity. In fact, we are told that suffering is okay, for like gold, our souls are refined in fire and inevitably we will come out purer, stronger, and better than we were before. When I lie in bed at night and believe that I'm going to start hallucinating, I rebuke the Devil instead, and it does provide momentary relief. I ask for extra prayers in my weekly Bible study class. The Bible study leader takes me to a bishop on a Thursday afternoon, and he prophesizes that he sees me standing in front of a mirror as my skin peels off my bones and falls to the ground like feathers. He tells me that I'm going "through it," and I need to do something—anything—or else I'm going to find myself in a ravine out of which I cannot climb.

But this is good, I think. I need to suffer. I'm being refined. I'm going to come out good as new sooner or later. Maybe this whole process is lasting longer than I thought because I'm not learning some sort of lesson that God is trying to teach me. When I pray about it, I do feel a peace overwhelm me and settle my anxiety. But my moods still fluctuate, drifting from one extreme to the other. As soon as I rise to my feet again after kneeling down in prayer, I feel as if I could easily plummet right back to the ground in anguish. I train myself to think that this sensation means that my dependence on God is getting stronger and that this is a good thing. After all, if I don't have a relationship with God, then I can't call myself a true Pentecostal. I am powerless because I believe I need to be. I expect to wake up one morning and find the grieving over. Then, I'll testify to my community about how no one could have delivered me but God.

And then my prayers start to grow stagnant, and I don't know what to do.

About a week before the premiere of the play I co-wrote, my mother calls me and, in a calm voice, says that my stepfather does not have much time left. I have to come to the hospital to see him. He has been refusing to eat and drink for a few weeks, but he is not afraid. When my grandmother sits in a chair by his bed, she exuberantly sings hymns and he claps his hands or moves his head from side to side. When my grandfather preaches to him about rededicating his life to Christ before his mind and body go, my stepfather looks up to the ceiling and lifts his hands, an action that we all believe means he is ready to be taken home.

When I visit him in his hospital bed, I am not afraid. My mother tells me that although his eyes are closed and his mouth is open, he can hear anything I want to say. I tell him that I love him, and that I thank him for being such a blessing in my life and my mother's. The corners of his mouth curve upward and I interpret this as a smile. He hears me. He loves me. He can understand. I am reminded of when I visited him by his bedside to tell him about getting into Princeton and that I would have to pay close to nothing. His dementia was already advancing by then, but he had smiled and said, in a clear tone, "I'm not surprised." It was like he remembered everything. He had always believed in my intellect and beauty, and always encouraged me. I felt as if I had a stepfather again. He was still present. I reconceived of his mind as one that goes in and out. When it returns, it sends a message that has me believing in magic—or God's grace—and the beauty of life all over again.

Later on, after I have left, my mother whispers to him that it is okay to leave, and he does. When I get the news, I'm not sure if I still want to go back to Princeton to see the opening night of my play. I think it is inappropriate to leave, even cruel, but my mother urges me to go. I have been working on it throughout my sophomore year, and fighting with other more popular, white-dominated arts groups to get the performance space that the production deserves. I listen to her and return to campus. The show sells out. People agree to pay half price to sit on the steps to watch. My collaborators and I could only have dreamed of this several months ago. Although my mother cannot make it and my stepfather has already passed, my father, Mathurin, shows up front and center. Growing up, I desired nothing more than to make him proud, and now his eyes are glimmering as my art comes alive in front of his face. His presence reinforces to me how loved I am. I am happy.

To my surprise, it was my mother who suggested, a few months before my stepfather passed, that I go to therapy. She had been researching for days leading up to one of my breaks from college, and made my first appointment. She told me that I would be fine, and that she would sit alongside me if I authorized it.

My first thought was: *If she thinks it's okay, then it must be okay.* My mother is one of the most religious people I know, and I still look to her for counsel. She told me that I needed to get well, not to be like some other parishioners in our church who suffered from psychological and physical distress yet refused to seek help.

At first I sat and fidgeted on a comfy sofa while obsessively looking at the clock. But soon, I felt like weights were being taken off my heart. I finally had someone to talk to about my feeling of weakness without the fear of being embarrassed. I realized that it was okay to admit out loud that I'm weak, I'm tired, I'm hurt, and some days, I am not happy. As a black woman studying at an Ivy League university, I felt like I had to put on a facade of perfection all the time, or else I was not meant to be at such a prestigious institution—a space that was never originally meant for people like me. Whenever I went home, my family members reminded me how much of a blessing it was. I wasn't supposed to be unhappy, and if I was, I should just suck it up.

I saw the therapist a few times before and after my stepfather's death. She recognized that I needed to restructure my thought process, and none of her methods deviated from or challenged what I knew to be true within the tenets of my religion. The guilt of being disobedient to God gradually faded. There is a time to pray and there is a time to act. My soul did not have to be at odds with either, and I wish that others like myself would recognize this when they cry for help. I felt peace in my head and in my bones.

After my stepfather passed, my mother herself hovered on the verge of depression. She would not leave her bed, and all the curtains in the house were closed. Taking care of him had taken a huge toll on her, as it would on anyone. She was exhausted from watching his every move, and infuriated that his colleagues had never called or come around to check up on him. She gained over a hundred pounds from stress. But she never viewed him as a burden. He was her husband. She never complained. She didn't so much as wince or groan when she had to get up to take him to the bathroom, or bathe him. This is the most extreme example of love that I will probably ever witness in my life.

I pushed her to go to a support group at a hospital that was just ten minutes away in a neighboring town. She went and returned home a more revitalized woman, and she kept going to the sessions. She lost those hundred pounds, and then some more. And eventually, I did not pace; I did not check, double-check, triple-check, quadruple-check, sextuple-check, septuple-check, octuple-check anything; I did not wake up in a panic in the middle of the night, or fear that a bell was going to fall from the sky and pulverize me. I still experience infrequent waves of apprehension around silverware, not because I want to harm myself but rather because my reflection in the metal utensils reminds me that I am still here. I am living.

At times I do feel quivers of compulsion. I keep thinking that I'll forget an alarm, but I never do. I think something will catch on fire, but it never does. I am learning to trust myself more and in turn work less, which is still more than enough. I do not know if OCD will become a constant in my life, if what I went through was just a one-time experience or the first glimpse of a condition that I will have to battle in synchronicity with the ebbs and flows of my life.

I DID NOT REALIZE AT FIRST THAT PSYCHOLOGICAL HEALING was in fact what I needed more than anything after my surgery. My mother had reluctantly brought me back to Harlem, but I still could not wipe myself after using the bathroom, only pat. I could not wash my vagina as usual, but rather let the soapsuds slide down my body. I could not laugh as raucously as I used to; laughing required me to hold my stomach up and space out my giggles so that I would not feel pain from the stitches. I had to sit with pillows underneath me. And then the dreams started. I had feverish dreams in which I would be walking down the street when a man would push me up against a wire fence before loosening his belt buckle. I would tell him that I was physically unable to be penetrated, but he would force himself in anyway. My stitches would rip and I would go into shock. When he'd finished, my rapist would kick me there for good measure before disappearing into the night. Every dream I had was about sexual assault, although the focus was less on me being penetrated without my consent and more on my stitches being torn out. I felt less like a woman and more like a rag doll that could come undone at any moment.

My journal pages filled with my frantic thoughts. I feared that if anyone read it, they would assume that I was having a mental breakdown. When I walked to the train station I had to remind myself to act as I had done prior to my procedure, because every force inside of me wanted me to pull down my pants and yell at everyone to look at what a doctor had done to me. I didn't care about being catcalled, about a man getting hard, about a mother shielding her child's eyes. I needed to experience some emotion, some sensation, other than pain. I tried masturbating, but after forty-five minutes I was still hardly wet. Before, I could come in less than fifteen.

The man who I was dating at the time wanted to see me. When we got back to his place, after a glass and a half of wine, I was taking my top off. We quickly moved from the living room to his bedroom, but I just wanted to be next to another body when I could barely hold on to my own. As he pressed up against me, I hissed and told him to be gentle. I was still in recovery, after all.

And that's when he asked, "Can I see it?"

"See what?"

His eyes dropped below my waist, and so I showed him. He could have stared at me for three minutes or an hour. I was so focused on how this was one of the most intimate experiences of my life. I didn't need to be penetrated. I had never been. All I needed was to be reminded that I was still a woman.

MY VAGINA ISN'T AND WAS NEVER A "FLOWER." MY VAGINA was a labyrinth. I had to strategize and maneuver, pushing excess flesh around, to see all that I contained. I would watch episodes of *Baywatch*, *Sex and the City*, *Girls*, and *Degrassi*, and wonder why no one ever talked about vaginas unless it was in relation to birth or periods. What about oversized labia? What about their pain? What about our pain? I wrote a much shorter essay about my labiaplasty for *Fusion*, an assignment that my mother warned me against out of fear that I would turn off potential suitors. I didn't tell my father until several months after my procedure. I don't know if he even remembers me telling him. My friends found out about a month post-op; I didn't tell them beforehand because I was ashamed. I felt like I was breaking some ancient feminist creed that maintains that we have the bodies we have, and if we manipulate them, the patriarchy is destroying us. I didn't tell them because much of my femininity had been wrapped in secrecy and pain, and the further pain born of secrecy.

I do not regret my surgery. I do not praise it either. My pain is gone. When I part my legs now, I have to remind myself of what used to unfurl. However, there are some spots that are still sensitive, spots where I am not entirely certain that the stitches have disintegrated. I do not know if this is a psychosomatic response, some remnants of my feverish dreams perhaps, but I don't need to know. I am content, and that is all I need.

7

HUMAN, NOT BLACK

THERE WAS CHAOS AT HOME AND IN MY HEART AS MY STEPFA-
ther's health declined, but I found solace in the dizzying
prose of Dostoyevsky, in the way he made madness seem
almost normal, even attractive. I read his novella *The Double*,
in which a man is convinced he has a doppelgänger, then
Crime and Punishment, in which a man kills an old pawn-
broker and believes himself to be superior to anyone else. I
regaled myself with the long, drawn-out psychological conversations in *The Brothers Karamazov.* In a matter of months
I became a fanatic, and I decided to learn the language—I
wanted to know what lay beyond the barrier of translation,
to discover the untranslatable intricacies of Dostoyevsky's
work. As a comparative literature major, I had to learn at least
two foreign languages to graduate. I'd already chosen Japa-

nese, and I'd been flirting with the idea of French because I loved *Madame Bovary*. But Russian seemed more daring. It turned out to be a much harder conquest than Japanese: the verb conjugations seemed contradictory, the linguistic logic impenetrable, the pronunciation coarse. However, after hard work, I was accepted into an intermediate Russian course at the Nevsky Institute in St. Petersburg held during the summer following my sophomore year.

After I got in, I was told by both the program's director and my introductory Russian teacher that there had been a rise in hate crimes there over the past few years, and if I had any reservations about going, they would understand. I wondered if they told this to my peers. I was not the only person of color—there was Jacqueline, a Singaporean woman, and Daniel, a Mexican-American guy—but I was the only black person. Ultimately, I decided to go anyway; immersing myself in the culture, I thought, and hearing the language buzzing in my ears all summer was the only way to truly learn.

I ARRIVED IN ST. PETERSBURG ON MY TWENTIETH BIRTHDAY. After I landed, a Nevsky Institute representative took me to my host family's apartment on Krasnogo Kursanta ("Red Cadet") Street in the Petrogradskaya District. Their building was next to a courtyard, but on the inside it felt abnormally dark. I would be rooming with Jacqueline, an arrangement I assumed was intentional because we were both women of color. Our host mother was a part-time singer who regularly had international guests, from American to Indonesian, shuffling in and out of her apartment. She had two children, a son and daughter—I believe their names were Misha and Sasha—and I could count on my fingers how many times I actually saw them. I'd hear their voices, but I never bumped into them while passing through the corridor. They could have been apparitions for all I knew. Jacqueline and I would eat together at the dining table—we never shared meals with the family. We would never be integrated into this family because our being there was strictly business.

I took the room closest to the front door. A portrait of Alexander Pushkin hung on the wall outside my bedroom. Because Russians pride themselves on their literature perhaps more so than any other facet of their culture, Pushkin is held in the same esteem as Americans hold Elvis Presley, or the English the Beatles. You can probably stop a Russian child on the street and ask him or her to perfectly recite one of Pushkin's poems. I found it interesting that this man, whose African heritage I could detect in his nose and around his jawline, was so revered here and yet black people like myself were not.

To be fair, my treatment in St. Petersburg was far milder than that experienced by other black people. I've heard stories of people having things thrown at them, being harassed on the metro, having children point at them as if they were carnival freak show exhibits. However, the threat of danger was everywhere. In Russia, if you are a foreigner, you will be stared at unblinkingly for close to a minute with an intensity I will never forget. I remember countless moments when I was on the escalator at Chkalovskaya station while a Russian—most times, a man—was unable to take his eyes off of me. In my prior experience, a held gaze meant attraction, but this was different. His entire face would be stoic and his eyes would be unyielding even after he knew that I knew that he was watching me. I would look down at my copy of *The Master and Margarita*, look up, and he would be staring at me. I would scrape out the dirt from under my fingernails, look up, and he would be staring at me. I would check my cell phone for any messages from my classmates, look up, and he would still be staring at me. I couldn't tell him how rude it was to stare because my vocabulary was limited. I would stutter, and he would know that he had the upper hand in more ways than one. So I remained dejected and uncomfortable, under surveillance all the time.

It took about two to three weeks for me to be okay with riding the metro by myself. I expressed my anxiety to grad students who accompanied us on the trip. They were sympathetic, but they didn't really get it; it wasn't their experience. Unlike me, they could roam around freely. One time I did take the metro downtown alone, to meet a Russian "friend" assigned by the institute to help me acclimate to St. Petersburg, and a man said hello to me in Russian as I was gathering tokens for the ride. I did not like his tone. His voice was low and his face cold, like the others', yet he seemed hungry for something. He stood a few steps behind me on the escalator, and I pretended to occupy myself with games on my phone. Once the train arrived, I hopped on and he got into the same car. Something wasn't right, and I could feel it. A blond-haired man sitting on the opposite side of the car leaned forward and stared at me, and I began to feel like they were in it together, that finally all of this staring would come to a head. Two large men were gathering their suitcases to get off at Admiralteyskaya, my stop, so I slipped in between them. Unfortunately, the man who had been following me did a double take and slipped out before the doors closed. I began to walk briskly. I had to make it to the station entrance, where there would be the safety of hundreds of people around. Then again, how would he lose me? I was black. I couldn't find a police officer because I didn't have the vocabulary to properly articulate my concern, and even if I did, would the officer care?

STUDENTS FROM THE UNIVERSITY OF EDINBURGH IN SCOT-land were also studying at the Nevsky Institute that summer. During one of our afternoon breaks, we were given the chance to visit the classroom across the hall and meet them. Daniel and I quickly established a rapport with them. We were drawn to their free-spirited and easygoing personalities. Michael was a gay man who towered over six feet, Catherine was a short blonde, and Emily was a long-haired brunette whose natural drawl signaled to me that she partied hard. We agreed to hang out, along with Daniel's Russian "friend" Anastasiya, at Mishka Bar, which was not too far from Nevsky Prospekt, the main thoroughfare in the city. Underground and badly lit, it was a hipster spot decorated in gray and pink, frequented by plenty of twenty-somethings and expats. When I walked in, I didn't feel so self-conscious. It was the first moment when I felt like I could relax and pretend that I was not different from anyone else. I ordered a Long Island iced tea to loosen up even more. Who knew when I would return to Russia, a country that's famously known for its vodka? I might as well go hard, I thought. Because I had never had a Long Island iced tea, I underestimated its power, and by the time I returned to our spot in the back of the bar, the side of my face was already on the table. Catherine and Emily giggled at how drunk I was before talking to some locals, who invited them to come to another bar. We figured that we should all go as a group, and the bar they suggested was not too far from Mishka.

I don't remember where we turned; all I knew was that the street was suddenly less populated than the riverside embankment outside Mishka Bar. A group of young Russian men was hanging around on the sidewalk, and one of them pinned me against the wall of a building. He smirked at me, and because his eyes weren't focusing I knew that he was drunk. I stayed still and said nothing. There wasn't enough time to be afraid. As soon as I realized that it was probably not wise for me to try to escape from underneath his arms, Michael gently grabbed me and escorted me to the bar, which was a hole-in-the-wall on the second floor of some building.

The woman at the door checking IDs examined my face more than my driver's license and asked, "You from America?"

When I told her yes, she said, "Good luck," and handed me back my license.

Believing that she did not know how to say "Have a good time" or "Enjoy" in English, I took her response as a well-wish rather than a warning.

By this time, I had somehow sobered up, but Daniel was beyond drunk. We had lost Catherine and Emily from the moment we turned the corner onto the street, but given the smallness of this new bar, we felt sure that we would find them inside soon. It was much dirtier and less attended by internationals than Mishka. After about a half hour of circling around, we saw both Catherine and Emily sitting beside some Russian men, dressed in all black, with shaved heads. Michael, who was also very inebriated by this point, decided to approach one of them. I stood farther back, my body disappearing behind his.

Michael stuck out his hand and one of the men shook it before saying, "Do you know what I am? I'm skinhead."

Immediately, I pivoted and grabbed Daniel's hand. He tried to resist, but I gripped his wrist tighter and we flew down the staircase. In that moment of fight-or-flight, I couldn't feel my feet hitting the steps or the pavement outside. Once we were out in the open air, Anastasiya joined us, visibly concerned but her mind congealed by alcohol. Daniel drunkenly yelled at me, asking me why we were outside, and I told him that there were neo-Nazis. His face dropped, but he was so drunk I didn't know if he'd fully understood what I said. I dragged both him and Anastasiya into a nearby Subway sandwich shop, and we sat there until the Edinburgh students joined us. Michael was quiet, but Catherine and Emily were giggling as they recounted the men and their Nazi saluting—they said they had joined in. They said that they'd done it because they were afraid, but their faces suggested otherwise. I began to wonder if this was just another raucous night for them, a crazy story that they could afford because they were white.

We were in the same city where three Zambian students had been severely beaten, one left in coma, just a few months before we arrived. Several years earlier, Lamzar Samba, a fifth-year student from Senegal at Saint Petersburg State University of Telecommunications, was shot dead as he left a club with his friends. A hunting rifle decorated with a swastika was found at the scene. As I sat in that Subway shop, thoughts of what could have happened to both me and Daniel swirled in my head. We could have been severely beaten. I could have been raped. We could have been left half dead on the street outside that hole-in-the-wall bar and the police would have taken us to jail, and once we came to, the officers would have said that we were damaging St. Petersburg's reputation with our Western hooliganism. When I explained to the Edinburgh students just how afraid I was, their laughter subsided. Their eyes expressed concern. They were sympathetic, but they weren't capable of true empathy—this fear wasn't theirs to know.

As white people, they could never fully understand. Sure, they might have realized that I could have been targeted because I was black. But that understanding is an abstraction. When it is contained within your black body, well, that is different in a way they will never be able to wrap their heads around, because they don't have to.

IN 1964, *HARPER'S MAGAZINE* PUBLISHED AN ESSAY CALLED "Harlem Is Nowhere," which Ralph Ellison had written nearly two decades earlier, in 1948. The inspiration for his piece was a trip he'd taken to the first mental hygiene facility in Harlem, the Lafargue Mental Hygiene Clinic, where black residents could receive care for twenty-five cents. Located in a church basement, the clinic and its staff, who worked for free, hoped to provide clients the tools they needed to survive in a hostile world. The essay begins, "To live in Harlem is to dwell in the very bowels of the city; it is to pass a labyrinthine existence among streets that explode monotonously skyward with the spires and crosses of churches and clutter underfoot with garbage and decay." Ellison observed that, in Harlem, a common response to "How are you?" was "Oh man, I'm *nowhere*," signaling the speaker's lack of a stable position in society.

When I first moved to Harlem, I found a summer gig teaching first- and second-generation Chinese students who wanted to test into elite prep schools. The job was in southwest Brooklyn, and my subway commute was an hour each way. I would try to carve some kind of private space for myself during that time by reading books and sticking my earbuds in so deep that I believed that everything was the soundtrack of my own biopic. I learned early on that if you want to be invisible in New York City, it is very easy. Someone may be sitting next to you on the train, but you can squeeze your body so far into itself that you can fool yourself into believing that you alone have the whole row of seats. Homeless people and hopeful rappers may call out to you on the street, but you can walk past them without so much as turning your neck. Then there are the people who do not want to be invisible, who will do everything to bridge the gap between public and private spaces.

One morning soon after I'd moved, I got on the subway to ride downtown and a black woman was standing near the side of my train car, opposite the sliding doors. She was gently swiveling and placing all her weight on her right hip.

Her jaw jutted outwards; her lips were pursed. I thought she was sucking on a Sour Patch Kid, or maybe she had to go to the bathroom. Beside her, a youthful, grungy-looking white guy with his hair in disarray was playing with some kind of electronic device.

Out of nowhere, this black woman began talking to him about Jesus in a thick West Indian accent: "Ya hafta repent to di Fatha for all yuh sins. Him comin back soon."

She spoke to him with such assertion that I assumed they knew each other and he was intentionally ignoring her. She continued to go on and on about how this white man needed to take heed of Jesus's imminent return. He rolled his eyes and walked to the other side of the car as the woman continued to warn not only him but now everyone else on the train to get right.

I thought that this woman must be a lunatic. To be fair, I think every person living on the island of Manhattan harbors some degree of madness. We're all crowded together in small spaces, and we need to claim something out in the open as our own by any means necessary. The vast majority of us are crammed into apartments that we cannot afford, and every day we bunch into the subway, our energies boomeranging off one another. (An Afro-Cuban woman from Brooklyn advised me to wash each night to rid myself of the accumulated energy from all the people I unconsciously interacted with on the subway, and then rub peppermint oil on my skin for good measure.) In the weeks immediately after my move, I would feel exhausted after riding the subway, even if I'd only gone from Harlem to midtown and back on a short errand. Once I saw a man on the 2/3 train talking to himself, very loudly, about all the slaughter and pestilence in the Old Testament. He ended with each sentence with an emphatic "*sick*." Then, he snapped back into sanity when he apologized to the woman beside him for hitting her with his belongings. I have seen young men rap aloud on crowded trains; countless people play music on their phones without using headphones. All of these people riding to and from Harlem on the subway—the majority of them black, a small portion Latinx—seemed a little bit unhinged to me.

I HAD NEVER LIVED IN A PREDOMINATELY BLACK SPACE BEFORE moving to Harlem. For as long as I can remember, I have been taught to not embarrass my mother with certain kinds of behavior and styles of dress, and to not act "simple." She never said this, though, when we were in a black church, at a black cookout, at a black anything. It was only a warning issued when I was going out into the wider white world, in which blackness and all of its inexplicable grooves are suppressed. Unless I was in a space that was totally black, my dialect had to be modulated, my gesticulations moderated, my voice quieted, my hair tamed, my clothes fastened. This is what I considered proper. This is what I considered normal. If I wanted to achieve any kind of success, I first had to recognize that success was a white domain and that if I did not adhere to its rules, then I would never go anywhere. Not in no literary world. Especially not in no New York.

The thing was, when I moved to Harlem, I ain't know shit, and I was not prepared for how far out of my element I would be there. My brain had assembled images of Harlem like a collage of black history, yet none of these images were congruent with one another. I knew of the Cotton Club and the Apollo, James Baldwin and Billie Holiday, crack cocaine and crime. Having been educated in majority-white spaces, I was guilty of reducing my own culture. These images brushed up against one another, inevitably fraying one another's edges. I couldn't get used to the block parties that lasted far past midnight, the arguments underneath my window at two a.m., the rap music blaring on the corners. I couldn't understand why black men sat on crates in front of barbershops and hat stores all evening, why black women and men sold sweet potato pies and incense on the street at 125th and Lenox if those same items were being sold in stores one block over, why everyone spoke so loudly that everyone knew everyone else's business. I was the same race as my neighbors, but I was not from the same culture.

In fact, I felt closer to my white, gay, Republican roommate than anyone else—at least I thought I did. Thomas had lived in Harlem for a decade and witnessed our block change dramatically. Former roommates had been robbed at gunpoint, but now I could walk home at two a.m. and find no other entity on the street besides a stray cat. The mantelpiece in our living room was stacked with his books, their authors ranging from James Joyce and Georg Hegel to Harriet Ann Jacobs and James Baldwin. We quickly established a rapport over our shared love of literature and trap music. We spoke frequently about gentrification. He firmly believed that if it weren't for gentrification, neither of us would be living in Harlem. I began to wonder if perhaps, in a place like Harlem, I exerted the same amount of damage as a white person like

Thomas did. If somehow he and I were both gentrifiers because we were college-educated and upwardly mobile.

I WAS SO INTRIGUED BY THE IDEA THAT I COULD BE BOTH black and a gentrifier that I wrote an article about it for the *Guardian*, which went viral. Some readers praised me for my introspection, and others judged me for being lazy and not contributing to my environment, an accusation that was true to an extent. I had never even gone to a block association meeting. Most of my friends were those whom I'd met at Princeton. Most of the places I frequented were upscale restaurants and bars like Cove Lounge, Corner Social, Sylvia's, and Red Rooster. I partook in a carefully curated version of life in Harlem.

But I didn't write the piece out of a feeling of superiority; I wrote it because I felt confused. I became less sure that the people I saw expressing themselves on the subway were unhinged because I realized I had always used white behavior as a reference point. I did not know how to live in a black space. I did not know where to start, or who could teach me. I was trying to learn behavior that should have been instinctive, behavior that I had been conditioned to see as outside of the norm. Now, in Harlem, this behavior was spread across my world like jam on toast. It was forcing me to tear myself apart, a persona that had been forged in my New Jersey upbringing and on trips abroad, and be free. But I pathologized that freedom. In my heated conversations about police brutality and blackness with Thomas, he would always want me to state facts and sources, explain my reasoning, and he would launch into a harangue when my responses were not to his liking. Each time I would walk away feeling as if my blackness had been whittled down like wood. I realized that that closeness I felt with him was duplicitous and in order to see Harlem, to really see and understand her for myself, I had to shut him out.

ONE OF THE CRITICS OF MY *GUARDIAN* PIECE TURNED OUT TO be my next-door neighbor, a black man named Alexander who had lived in the area for almost twenty years. He sent me a private message on Facebook, asking if we could meet up for smoothies. At first, I was afraid. According to his page, Alexander was a part of the Manuscripts, Archives and Rare Books Division at the Schomburg Center, one of the leading institutions of black culture in the world. In my article I'd declared that, despite being black, I felt a separation from Harlem, and I assumed that meeting with him would only make me feel more alone. I expected that he wanted nothing more than to eviscerate me, calling my work ahistorical and irrelevant over a nice strawberry-banana smoothie with a wheatgrass shot.

He told me to meet him in front of the lobby at the Schomburg, less than ten blocks from my apartment. A few minutes after I got there, I saw a bald, light-skinned black man emerge from the door. He wore thick-rimmed glasses, and had a goatee and a dignified smile. After grabbing our smoothies from a small shop around the corner, he took me back to the Schomburg, a place that holds Langston Hughes's ashes, signed documents from Toussaint Louverture, and a rare recording of a Marcus Garvey speech. Over ten million objects of the black diaspora are stored there.

Alexander led me down to the courtyard, where we spoke about what it meant to be black, especially in a place like Harlem. He told me that he had wanted to meet me in person because, although he thought my article was interesting, he found it to be incomplete and knew that there had to be more behind my words. He was right. At the time, I hadn't been able to pick apart all my constantly shifting thoughts about who I was, and what Harlem meant to me.

Towards the end of our rendezvous, Alexander matter-of-factly declared, "Blackness is everything." It was there in that courtyard where I began to see my neighborhood through a new lens. Blackness was everything. Harlem was everything. Neither Harlem nor blackness could exist in a bubble, in a pocket that I only turned inside out when I boarded the train uptown. It had to be my everything. My everywhere. Harlem was everywhere.

ABOUT FOUR MONTHS AFTER PUBLISHING THAT GENTRIFICA-tion piece, after I published my first piece on *The New Yorker*'s Page-Turner, I received an email from Augustyna, a warm Polish woman who had been one of my biggest academic supporters as the undergraduate administrator of the Comparative Literature Department at Princeton. She'd left the school before I turned in my thesis, and besides a fortuitous crossing of paths during commencement weekend, when she'd met my parents, I had not seen her since, and I missed her. She asked if I would like to come to her home, a Dutch

Colonial farmhouse situated in Somerset County, for lunch, and when I accepted she explained that her beloved husband was significantly older than her, and she was his caregiver. I told her not to worry; my mother was my late stepfather's caregiver, and so I could understand what to expect. Relieved, Augustyna wrote back to say that her aunt and uncle would also be coming for lunch. They were interested in getting to know me, a student whom Augustyna had talked about, and they often visited their niece.

I had some preparation of my own to do. I stood in front of my freestanding mirror and undid my bun, letting my tight curls graze my shoulders. These were elderly European people after all, and I was worried that my naturally curly afro would be interpreted as too militant, or as a statement in the context of my politically charged articles. As a black woman, I feel it is one thing for me to wear my hair out in an afro when I am in public and interacting with people of many different backgrounds. It is quite another when I am invited to a white person's home. I didn't want to make Augustyna, her husband, or her aunt and uncle uncomfortable. Furthermore, I didn't want to expend mental energy on figuring out how to maneuver away if anyone tried to reach and pet my hair. I eventually decided to moisturize my hair with water and shea butter before pinning it back into a bun, with some of my curls hanging to the side.

As soon as I descended the steps of the New Brunswick station, I could see Augustyna smiling through the windshield of her black truck. It was a gloomy, rainy day, but I had to restrain my excitement as I crossed a busy intersection to reach her. Her dirty-blonde hair was in loose curls, seemingly untilled by the bristles of a brush or comb, accentuating her easygoing personality. Exhaustion peeked through the inner corners of her eyes, but her charming smile reassured me that I did not have to apologize for being an extra burden.

Augustyna's home was situated near a river. As we drew nearer, she suggested that I look through the passenger window at all of the farmhouses perched on acres upon acres of land. Apparently the area was famous for playing a part in the Revolutionary War, but all I could think about was how many black servants might have worked in each house, and where they would have lived.

As soon as Augustyna pulled up and turned off the truck's engine, her aunt opened the front door and yelled for us to hurry and get out of the rain. No taller than I was at five feet, she had short brown hair, an infectious and constant laugh, and a thick Polish accent. Her husband was her foil in both appearance and demeanor—he was medium height. She greeted me with a hug, but he stood in front of me, emotionless, while his cold blue eyes fixated on my face. I nervously smiled and said hello; then Augustyna's aunt tugged at her husband's arm and said, "Say something to her in Russian. She speaks Russian. Say something to her in Russian."

He held up his right hand, and she said no more.

My skin constricted. I had studied the language for four years, traveled to the country, and could even read medical science and technology articles without using a dictionary. I could handle whatever he threw at me, but I did not trust that he would be easy on me. He might pepper his sentences with archaic words not taught in Russian classes, and if I did not respond quickly enough he would think that I was a liar.

But instead he said, "I read your articles."

My shoulders dropped. "Oh yeah?" I replied in a perky voice as we made our way to Augustyna's living room, where her aunt relentlessly urged me to drink white wine.

Augustyna's husband didn't seem as sick as she'd implied. He was the one asking me the majority of questions about my work, my time at Princeton, and my reasons for getting into writing. All the while, the aunt was urging me to drink more, to drink more. I had nothing else in my stomach besides cornflakes and I worried that I would become tipsy before lunch was ready. The uncle barely said anything to me, just sat upright in his chair, his blue eyes unyielding. While Augustyna set the table in the dining room, I regaled the three of them with my deep dive into multiple languages, my travels to Japan, and my time in St. Petersburg. I made sure that I pulled my jaw back so that my mouth could not move too freely, allowing my voice to spill over with too much passion. I decorated the middles and ends of my sentences with flashy smiles and strained to keep my hands from making too many associative gesticulations. Augustyna's aunt and husband were visibly impressed by all that I had accomplished, but I can't recall her uncle even sipping the glass of wine that was in front of him. He was too preoccupied with studying me. I had become accustomed to that kind of stare when I was in Russia, and I knew how to carry on in spite of the scrutiny.

After Augustyna called us into the dining room, her aunt sat on my left and her uncle on my right. As I placed pear-

and-arugula salad and some vegetables on my plate, he finally spoke.

"Morgan, I am sorry for not talking much. It's just that you confuse me."

I shot a glance at Augustyna, whose cheeks were reddening even as she smiled to ease the tension. "I confuse you? How do I confuse you?" I chuckled and picked at my plate.

"Forgive me for what I am about to ask. I'm not from here. I've lived here for many years and worked as a doctor. I have been around plenty black men, but you are the first black woman who I have ever met. It's just that I don't understand why you would want to call yourself black. Why not just call yourself a human? Now, it is obvious that you are a woman. But do you have to be a black woman? Why can't you be a human?"

If I had been in the middle of swallowing a pear slice, it would have caught in my throat. I listened to the smooth violin music playing in the background and chuckled again—smiling, too, of course. I was not offended. I was stunned.

Augustyna interjected. "Morgan, you have to forgive my uncle. He's not from here and sometimes he says things that are . . ." Her voice tapered off.

"No, it's okay," I said. I twisted my upper body towards him and said, "I call myself a black woman because that's what I am. I can be both a black woman and a human. Those two identities aren't separate from each other."

"But why would you call yourself black?" he persisted. "To me, you are not black. You do not present yourself as a black woman, or at least the ones who I've heard about. You went to Princeton, you speak many foreign languages, you travel. If this were many decades ago, I might have married you."

I refused to make eye contact with Augustyna's aunt. Now the tension had escalated. Had his stare been underscored by his attraction to me, his inability to see me as both a black woman and a human, or both?

She chimed in, "She could've married our son! I mean, he's married now and has a kid but before, you know."

I suddenly lost my appetite. I continued to eat so that I would not be rude, but my embarrassment filled my stomach. I felt like chattel, as though I should have been *flattered* that I could have been acceptable as a wife for this man or his son. Marriage was something done to me, not a choice I made; a gift that a white man would deign to bestow because I met his standards. I wondered if he would have talked this way about me in front of his wife if I had been a white woman. I wondered if she didn't take offense because she was extremely confident in both herself and her marriage, or because I was black and black women could be shuffled like playing cards in the hands of white men.

At the same time, I wanted to be in his presence in order to expose him to someone different and force him to confront his own prejudices. It was unfathomable to me that he could have lived for four or five decades in America and never interacted with a black woman. If I had to be the first, so be it. But that was not what I'd signed up for when I agreed to come to Augustyna's home for lunch.

Augustyna's husband, in his jovial, unassuming, and indubitably British voice, added, "I don't understand why they are labels to begin with. We are all human. When I look at you, I see a human."

I thought that I might be interrogated about my arguments surrounding police brutality. I didn't think my hosts would suggest that black womanhood is diametrically opposed to humanity.

I THOUGHT ABOUT CHRIS FROM OKCUPID WHO SAID WHEN he saw my profile, he didn't see a "black woman," only a "woman." Between that experience and the one at Augustyna's home, I had been trapped in a paradox. These white men acted as if there was no difference between me and them, but in doing so they made it clear that I had to shed my identity as a black woman. I cannot be both perceived as a human and a black woman in their eyes because those two identities are incompatible with each other. My black womanhood cancels out my humanity because black womanhood is inhuman.

White people think it is a compliment when they do not "see" you as a black person. In their minds, black people embody the biggest clusterfuck of societal ills: out-of-wedlock pregnancies, single mothers, drug addicts, high school dropouts. They are robbers, killers, rapists, convicts, degenerates, vagabonds, couch potatoes. Their pants are always sagging, they talk too loudly, they can barely speak English correctly, they dance too sexually. They cannot assimilate to white society, and if they seem perfectly okay with eschewing it, then they are condemned to being black because in a white society, blackness only exists as a punishment. They do not understand that blackness doesn't undermine but rather vivifies our humanity.

In my experience, white people are the only ones who purport to advance equality through the erasure or rejection of marginalized people's identities, which signals to me that they have fooled themselves into believing that they are "unraced." This belief is false, because it is based on the idea that whiteness is the human standard and that furthermore, by virtue of them being white, they are the arbiters of humanity. The Three-Fifths Compromise, a clause in the US Constitution that allowed for a state to count three-fifths of each black person when determining population for legislative representation in the House of Representatives, is a prime example of racism at its crudest level. People can only access their humanity by casting away all identities that exclude them from this white standard.

I did not respond to Augustyna's husband's comment, instead stuffing more arugula in my mouth like a rabbit meddling in someone's garden patch.

The last question her uncle asked me was this: "Why do you only write about black people? Aren't you afraid of cutting yourself short? You're a smart girl. You can write about anything."

I quietly laid my fork down on my plate. "I love writing about black people, and no, I don't think I'm cutting myself short, especially when our narratives are often neglected or dismissed altogether."

Augustyna nodded, and we proceeded into another room for Polish tea and pastries.

ON THE RIDE BACK TO THE TRAIN STATION, AUGUSTYNA PRO-
fusely apologized for her uncle's behavior. She explained
that because of his bluntness, he is rarely invited to social
events, and whenever she invites people over to her home
they can become uncomfortable. I was partly relieved that
Augustyna was not defending her uncle, but I was also somewhat disappointed that she did not defend me more during
that conversation. Then again, what could she have done?
She was learning, too, intently watching me when I spoke.
Would I have liked it if she had tried to interject and given
her thoughts on an experience that was not hers? And we all
have (often older) family members who are "too far gone"
on certain issues, who have not been swayed by any kind of
new argument since the Kennedy administration. Accepting
this is a resignation and an act of self-preservation in order to
retain our peace and sanity by not expending intellectual and
emotional labor on those who haven't asked for it.

WHEN I WAS SIX YEARS OLD, MY MOTHER CAME HOME ONE
day with a *Sailor Moon* VHS tape. The case cover had a pink
background studded with a pair of cunning eyes, and centered in the middle of them was the long-haired blonde
Sailor Moon. Her raised right hand held a crescent moon
scepter in the air; her left hand was balled in a fist. Tuxedo
Mask, Sailor's long-term boyfriend, hovered above the glow
of her scepter, while Luna, her purple cat, stood in between
her legs, her tail wrapped around Sailor's right leg. I'm not
quite sure why my mother brought me that tape. I assume she
did because I was obsessed with pink, and that was the extent

of her thinking. I wasn't an anime fan. My mornings were spent watching traditional cartoons like *Hey Arnold!*, *The Angry Beavers*, *The Ren & Stimpy Show*, and *Rocko's Modern Life*. My nights were spent watching a mix of new shows like *All That* and *Kenan & Kel* and reruns of *The Brady Bunch* and *The Mary Tyler Moore Show*. It wasn't like I needed any more VHS tapes. I pretty much had all the movies from the "Disney Renaissance," and repeatedly watched them with the same excitement I would have if it were the first time.

Either way, as a child I couldn't turn down a gift— especially not one with a pink cover—so I promptly watched the first three *Sailor Moon* episodes, and that's how my affinity for Japanese culture began. My eyes beamed whenever I saw Sailor Moon transform in midflight, a dazzling array of colors enveloping her body. I clenched my hands into fists just as she did whenever she called for the power of the moon to help her fight her enemies. I swooned every time Tuxedo Mask assisted her in fights after she'd lost her confidence or her willpower to persevere. Instead of voraciously devouring Disney, I began to consume *Sailor Moon*, buying more VHS tapes featuring full-length episodes as well as movies. It was a solitary passion until I was around eight or nine and I found out that twins from my church, three years my senior, were just as big of fans as I was. Candace and I were more passive in comparison to Bianca, who could draw accurate depictions of all the Sailor Scouts, sometimes as we watched episodes together. She was much more knowledgeable about *Sailor Moon*, and it was through her that I was able to draw the connection between the show and Japan. It had never occurred to me before that "Usagi Tsukino" was a Japanese name and that Azabu-Juban, where *Sailor Moon* lived, was a posh Tokyo neighborhood. Unfortunately, once I realized how far away on a map Tokyo was from New Jersey, my connection to *Sailor Moon* shrank. This had less to do with the fact that she was a blonde-haired, blue-eyed Japanese teenager who looked nothing like me and more to do with the realization that I couldn't be with her because of how far away she lived. Sailor Moon was more real to me than any other animated character, and I wanted to be her friend.

However, I wasn't ready to give up on her yet. I decided to learn about Japan. I Google-searched images of Japan, my heart fluttering at the sight of Shibuya Crossing, traversed by millions of people every day as bright, neon buildings buzzed behind them. I watched Travel Channel specials on Tokyo and saw white women eating sushi cooked right in front of them at Tsukuji Fish Market, taking a subway ride that was free from rats and trash, and passing by cosplayers around Yoyoji Park near Harajuku station. To me, Japan seemed like a portal between the real and the surreal, and so it excited me more than any other place on earth. It was a place where talking trash cans moved through the streets as freely as people, robots were mistaken for humans, and cell phones could be used to pay for treats at vending machines.

I DIDN'T THINK THAT IT WAS POSSIBLE FOR ME TO VISIT JAPAN until I discovered the People to People Student Ambassador Program, which led a two-week excursion throughout many Japanese cities, such as Tokyo, Hiroshima, and Kyoto, and organized a two-day stay at a host family's home. I don't remember mine being a particularly friendly group of people. It was very cliquish, the factions easily discernible through where we sat on our tour bus. The farther back someone was, the more popular they were. I sat closer to the front, near the chaperones. I was the only black girl. There was one black guy, but we didn't even speak to each other until midway through the trip. One of the more popular white guys even asked me why I spoke so loudly while everyone else snickered. It seemed like the majority of them saw the trip to Japan not as a learning experience but as a vacation, and their raucous and frequently disrespectful behavior would often go without reproach. They would scoff when they patronized shops and restaurants and couldn't find a Japanese salesperson who spoke English. Some of them laughed while we spent the day at the Hiroshima Peace Memorial Museum, an experience that left me so traumatized that I couldn't sleep that night. The guys horseplayed around in an *onsen* (a Japanese bathhouse), disturbing the tranquility of the traditional *ryokan* (inn) in which it was located. I didn't feel like I established a rapport with anyone until halfway through the trip, and by that time I was more engrossed by Japan than by any person in the program.

From the moment we landed at Narita International Airport, I was in disbelief. I thought that the Japanese signs had been purposely hung to deceive me into believing that I was in Tokyo and not a much cleaner version of Manhattan. My body had found its way to the literal other side of the world, yet I saw not a single reflection of myself in anyone around me. I was treated with the utmost respect and fascination wherever I went. I wasn't ignored when I went into stores. I constantly received bows, which I reciprocated. Essentially, I forgot that I was black; I was simply a foreigner, a *gaijin*, and this was a relief even at fourteen years old. Yes, politeness and modesty are integral elements of Japanese culture, but they made me, a young black American girl, feel special.

On the long train ride to Matsuyama, where I was going to stay with a host family, I worried that separated from my mostly white group, I could no longer hide behind the simple identity of a *gaijin*; I would be seen and treated as a black girl, just as I had been my whole life. Much to my surprise, when I met the family of four, the father spoke to me in Japanese and, although I could only say *"Wakarimasen"* ("I don't understand"), I was delighted that he assumed that I was bilingual. My only regret is that I couldn't have stayed with that family longer. I discovered that they had been a host family for years, creating large scrapbooks celebrating the people who they've hosted, and those who have hosted them. The father was a businessman who left in the early mornings before I had breakfast and didn't return until I had my bath in the evening. The mother was a housewife who shuffled their daughter to violin lessons and their son to playdates. In between, she took me on shopping trips to local bazaars and events with other host families in the area. Matsuyama was described to me as the countryside, but I quickly learned that the Japanese countryside is not the same as rural America. I had expected few to no people, tumbleweed, banjos or mandolins playing from some imperceptible place. On the contrary, Matsuyama was the capital city of the Ehime Prefecture and contained *onsens*, castles, several universities, and art museums. There was, though, a small

Christian church not too far from a rice field, where I went with my host family, who were also Christian. On my last day, the daughter gifted me with a gimp bracelet that she stayed up every night to handcraft while I slept in her brother's bed. The whole family waved to me as my carrier transported me away. Years later, I still think about their warmth, and I wish that I could write to them. Because I couldn't speak Japanese at the time, their names and address have long since slipped away from me.

I NEVER FORGOT THAT FEELING OF PSYCHOLOGICAL LIBERA-tion, which is why when I enrolled at Princeton I immediately signed up for introductory Japanese courses. Rather quickly, I discovered that most of my fellow students already had some familiarity with the language: Chinese students who already knew all the *kanji*, or characters; those who had taken four years of Japanese in high school but could not place into a higher course in college; and a few Japanese-American students who could not read well, but spoke fluently. These students influenced the way in which tests were curved, and I, who only spoke Spanish at the time, felt like I was at a great disadvantage. My grades were fine, but I probably was one of the lowest-performing students in the class. I wasn't good at dictation, second-guessed myself with particles, and fumbled during role-plays while those who probably only had to study for exams the night before aced them. Towards the end of freshman year, we were encouraged to apply for a summer intermediate Japanese study program in Ishikawa Prefecture.

I didn't get accepted. Devastated, I fervently searched for another one, ended up at the Middlebury Language School at Mills College, and then studied some more after the program to make sure I learned the same material as those in the Ishikawa program. I placed into Advanced Japanese 301, but the demographics in this class were even less diverse: mainly white men and those of Asian descent. I was still one of the lowest-performing students on tests, but in conversation, I flexed my muscles. It was then that the freedom I'd felt in Japan flooded back to me, and I was much more improvisational and free-flowing than my classmates.

Each time I went to class, I felt enveloped by an entirely different culture and I relished the feeling. I wanted to become a polyglot, undermining stereotypes about black women, or maybe placing myself outside of them. No one would expect a black woman to have an advanced proficiency in Japanese; I could be part of more social situations, my multilingualism allowing my identity to be as shapeshifting as my tongue.

My passion for Japanese would carry me throughout my years at Princeton. As more and more students opted out of it—those same students who had surpassed me when we were underclassmen—I persevered. By the time I applied to become an intern at Temple University Japan's Institute of Contemporary Asian Studies—which was coincidentally located in Azabu-Juban, Sailor Moon's neighborhood—I was damn near conversationally fluent. I was able to tell the time and hold forth on the implications of an aging society with only slight hesitation. I was going to work with Mei Nakamura, an author and associate professor of creative writing and Japanese literature at the university, and Calvin Sanders, senior associate professor in the Department of Humanities at the International Christian University. I would work on my writing with Mei while helping Calvin translate modern and contemporary Japanese poetry with the intention of publication.

My return to Japan was a relief. Once I landed at Narita International Airport and found a shuttle to Ikebukuro, I huddled in my seat with my earbuds in, reading the Japanese signs. If I was going to seamlessly reenter this country, casting off the mantle of being a black American woman, my Japanese knowledge would make that much easier. I made a concerted effort to ignore updates about the ongoing trial of George Zimmerman, the man who fatally shot Trayvon Martin, a young black boy, for wearing a hoodie in a gated community. I spoke Japanese and made *purikura* with my black Middlebury alumni friends in Shinjuku; bathed in an *onsen* and took a cable car around Mount Fuji with my fellow interns in Hakone; dined with Japanese businessmen in Shibuya; frequented Japanese churches and museums in Roppongi. My mother and her boyfriend at the time visited me in Japan for my twenty-first birthday, and she was astounded that no matter which shop she entered in the Ginza district—Tokyo's version of Fifth Avenue—she was always asked if she needed help and no saleswoman hesitated to hand her an expensive purse to look at. Whenever we left a department store, she would tell me that she had never been treated with that much respect in an American store *ever*. For her, to be acknowledged upon entering a store and then allowed to peruse the aisles without being followed was intoxicating. I wanted to tell her that in Tokyo she was not a black American but simply an American, a *gaijin*, but I ultimately chose not to do so. I didn't want to hamper her experience with national and linguistic comparisons between the United States and Japan.

None of this is to say that I was not aware of my blackness in Japan. *Obasans*, middle-aged Japanese women, touched my waist-length Senegalese twists when they discovered that I spoke Japanese and were stunned to learn the number of hours it took me to complete the hairstyle. But to the best of my knowledge, that was the extent of it, even though I have heard of other black people experiencing far worse. I was not in a country where my ancestors had been enslaved. I was not stared at when I walked through different neighborhoods either in the day or the evening, no waitress gave me poor service, no one made any snide remarks about my body, and I never heard a racial slur. In short, I was free. Until I heard that George Zimmerman had been acquitted.

I was sitting in my room in my dorm. It was early in the afternoon, and I had just finished translating some of Hagiwara Sakutaro's poetry. Like most afternoons, I was using Twitter to catch up on all the breaking news. Immediately after logging in, I saw a photograph of George Zimmerman's gleeful face, looking up and smiling at his lawyer, on my news feed. I don't remember breathing as I read through hundreds, maybe thousands, of tweets from black users expressing their grief and sorrow for Trayvon Martin. It was a shock wave that reverberated throughout the world, but because I was so far from America, I felt a deep pain at not being around those who looked like me during this moment of collective mourning. The walls began to close in around me. The sun piercing through the windows became too bright for my eyes. There was no word in Japanese or English that could accurately encapsulate how much I was sinking on the inside. I confided in one of my friends, a woman of white and Chinese Malay descent, who was a passionate Democrat. Like me, she was appalled with the ruling. That relief in sharing my disappointment, however, was short-lived. Her anger was political; mine was personal. I needed someone black to talk to.

WHY WOULD I CALL MYSELF A BLACK WOMAN WHEN I COULD just be a human? Why?

Because when I walk out of my front door, I am not simply treated as a human being. I am treated as a black woman. I am both unconsciously and consciously aware of how others' biases kick in when they see me, and how their subsequent treatment of me differs from the way they might treat someone else who is not black and female. The responses I get when I report my treatment to other black women let me know that these behaviors are patterns. My experience flattens if I believe that I can freely roam this earth without thinking about how my body impacts where I will and will not be tolerated. When a white person asks a black woman why she cannot just be a human, he or she is asking, *Why can't you be like me? Why can't you partake in the humanity that I have as my birthright, even though I can rip that humanity away*

*from you by casting you out of our society if you do anything that I
don't like?*

WHEN THE GEORGE ZIMMERMAN VERDICT WAS ANNOUNCED,
I only had a short time left in Tokyo and my sadness clouded
my enjoyment of these last few days. Whenever I boarded the
train on the Saikyō Line, I was more aware of how Japanese
people are not comfortable with making eye contact with
gaijin. Whenever my eyes connected with a Japanese person's,
their eyes would drop to the floor, and that aversion began to
shred me like cheese against a grater. Could they not see me?
Of course they could, because looking away meant that they
knew that I was an outsider. But I wasn't just an outsider. I
was a black outsider, and I was also a woman. They had to
realize this. I stood out among the white expats, who were
mostly young white men who loved anime and fetishized
Japanese women and white women who could easily seduce
a wide array of Japanese men. They had to know. I *wanted*
them to, because not acknowledging me was a dismissal of
the body in which I lived. Then again, wasn't this what I'd
wanted, to flee to Japan to become merely a foreigner? Wasn't
this the whole purpose of my relationship with Japan, for it
to wrap me around its cherry blossom trees, stretch me far
across its expansive mountain ranges, and then squash me
into a two-dimensional image that could be splashed across
the television screens of Shibuya Crossing? Isn't this what I'd
wanted?

Everything became distorted. I walked around Shinjuku

and sneered at people taking selfies while making the peace sign with their fingers. How dare they be happy when a black child met his untimely death and his killer went unpunished? How dare they be happy while I was sinking? There were Nigerian men who hung around Shinjuku, and I had been told that they were notorious for scamming, robbing, and drugging naive tourists. I'd ignored their gaze until now, but after the verdict all I wanted was to get drunk off plum wine, hobble over to one of them with teary eyes, and beg them to hold me—whether in public or a nearby hostel—for a few hours. I wanted to press my black skin against another black person's black skin, breathe in synchronicity, and remember that we were alive and that this was resistance in and of itself. Each Japanese word I uttered felt like a spritz of salt and lemon juice on my tongue. I was a fraud, pretending that my education and multilingualism would somehow protect me from the ever-revolving cycle of black death. I should have seen all of this coming.

I could not sleep. Each time I laid my head upon my pillow, I imagined that Trayvon Martin was hiding in the corner and that he would emerge—with blood pouring out of his fatal wounds—to stand before me with a look of sheer disappointment. *How dare you sleep? You have several hours while I have eternity. It was not my time to go.* When I closed my eyes, I saw George Zimmerman's smiling face—only this time he was facing me and not the judge. In his pupils I could see the reflection of Trayvon's cold corpse lying on the pavement, a body transfixed on the Floridian ground by bullets, a body en route to see his Father. And in Zimmerman's smile, I would see that I was next, that the destruction had already begun.

I had to sleep with the lights on, and with a movie playing on my laptop, to get any semblance of rest. I didn't tell any of my friends on the program. I feared that they would think that I was losing my mind and would perhaps report me to our supervisor. Besides, I would be back on American soil soon enough.

When I returned to New Jersey, nationwide protests were under way. I saw black people my age standing outside in the sweltering heat for hours with signs, refusing to lower their eyes whenever a police officer surveyed their mobilization. I didn't go to any protests that year, although I would in late 2014, months after Eric Garner died. That is how grief and resistance works. It is a cycle, and a revolution never ceases for a black person, no matter where we are or which languages we speak.

AFTER THAT LUNCH AT AUGUSTYNA'S HOUSE, I BEGAN TO RE-assess the many different settings in which I was one of the only black people, if not *the* only black person, in a room. Are white people only able to talk to me if they've trained their minds not to see me as black? Is the only path to acceptance not breaking the fantasy that white people have of everyone's equality? I've never thought I was anything *but* human. My black womanhood does not cancel out my humanity. These are not facts that repel each other.

Physiologically, of course, we are all human. Socially, we dehumanize people of color daily. We judge their clothes, speech, hair, and education level as criteria for whether they have earned the right to be treated with common decency.

We use these same criteria to judge if they deserve to die at the hands of law enforcement, or men like George Zimmerman. Because the question that white people are asking is not *Why can't we all be human?*, but *Why can't you be like us?*

Before Harlem, I had never experienced a space where blackness was so real that I could taste it—the consistency of baked macaroni and cheese, the sweetness of yams, the smoothness of the surface of fresh corn bread. It fills me up and comforts me, but I understand that our relationship cannot be one-sided. I have started to go to block association meetings, to explore more parts of Harlem, to pay more attention to the politics surrounding me. Blackness is like an engine that needs constant oiling.

My judgment of the black people I saw on the train—the woman I thought was crazy for speaking about the Lord to a white man, the man who spoke of the book of Deuteronomy to all those who boarded at 125th and Lenox, the men who rapped aloud, the black youths who played music without headphones—was made inside the context of a white world, a world that is measured by reason and protocol according to white people at the expense of people of color. I did not know why black people couldn't keep to themselves, why they could not remain invisible, why they couldn't shut up, why they couldn't stop trying to bring others into their spaces. Harlem is not a white space, and so black people do not need to behave in a way white people find respectable. We cannot, and should not, have to live our lives according to traditions of Western European civilizations because they are not natural to us. We are intensely spiritual and communal. We are a feeling kind of people. We can drop into a song at any time—the right time—and be on beat. We use our whole bodies to convey feeling. No parts of ourselves are closed off to others, and especially not to the environment; our black spaces reaffirm our connection to nature, our reality.

I STILL DREAM OF JAPAN. WHENEVER I SEE A JAPANESE RESTAURANT, whenever my teeth sink into *onigiri*, whenever I see paper lanterns, I yearn for it like a long-distance lover. But the truth is, it's not that simple. Japan hasn't come around to accepting Ariana Miyamoto, a half-black, half-Japanese woman, as Miss Japan—because I suppose her brownness nullifies her nationality. I often wonder if this love affair will be different the third time around, if my newfound comfort in my own skin and ability to question all I see will make me privy to all the things that I did not want to see before. What then?

I call myself black because that is who I am. Blackness is a label that I do not have a choice in rejecting as long as systemic barriers exist in this country. But also, my blackness is an honor, and as long as I continue to live, I will always esteem it as such.

8

WHO WILL WRITE US?

She walks through the waters of Louisiana's Lake Pontchartrain with five women behind her. They are all dressed in white, and their hands are clasped together in front of their midsections. The sun is beginning to set; the sky is tinged with hues of blue, light gray, yellow, and magenta. Besides a branch, no other entity is in the water to detract from these women. No birds or planes fly overhead.

As they cross the shallower parts of the lake, their moving feet create ripples that expand and multiply. They walk slowly because they need to take their time. Their leader is "going through," as older black women used to say. She is "going through," an ambiguous phrase that sounds small but encompasses a wide range of experiences and emotions. The only way to *get* through is to go through, and so she and her black female companions have taken to the water. Enslaved blacks went through these same southern waters to escape captivity. They would submerge themselves in the water to throw the slave catchers' dogs off their trail. But this scene reaches back further than 1619, when the Dutch sold the first captured Africans to the colonists in Jamestown. Water is a part of the Dagara cosmological wheel, an element that focuses on healing and reconciliation. It is a belief system used to build identities and communities. This water is about reconciliation; water creates balance and restores peace. It is a conduit through which someone can see beyond her turmoil. Immersion in water represents rebirth across many major religions: a Christian baptism, a mikvah in Judaism, the release from the cycle of life and death for Hindus who bathe in the Ganges, the Islamic practice of *wudū*. This scene, when she crosses the waters of Lake Pontchartrain with five black women behind her, is called "reformation": *reformacion, reformationem, reformare,* an improvement, an alteration for the better. She is moving across landscapes and traveling through emotions, and we are privileged enough to journey alongside her. Her name is Beyoncé, and she is both who we thought she was and everything we were not prepared for her to be.

WHEN BEYONCÉ RELEASED HER *LEMONADE* SPECIAL FOR HBO in late April 2016, I was not ready. I have a tendency to avoid watching and listening to highly hyped releases at the same time as everyone else because I think that their often exaggerated anticipation and response will affect my viewing and/or listening experience. But I received an assignment from Elle.com to write about *Lemonade*, and because I was getting paid, I knew that I had to do it now and I couldn't allow those exaggerations to affect my judgment. I had been wowed by the release of "Formation" two months prior. I knew that Beyoncé would show that black people are humans who deserved to be treated as such: capable of rage and deserving of respect. As I watched *Lemonade*, however, I felt like I was being broken open and hollowed out like a gourd, which Beyoncé filled with her raw melodies of ancient heartbreak and grief.

I was mourning throughout the entire hour-long special. I mourned for a relationship that I'd never had. I mourned for a love that I'd never experienced. I mourned for sons I'd never birthed. I mourned for a marriage in which I was never bound, a man who had never united himself with me, good times that never transpired, bad times that did. I did not know if I was projecting or if, through *Lemonade*, I was tapping into some deeper, communal spirit passing through an invisible wavelength connecting me to the women who came before me, existed alongside me, and will come after I am gone. I was beside myself, and had no idea how I was going to form a cogent argument, let alone open the essay. The experience was similar to watching something in a foreign language that you understand, and yet as soon as you feel those words with your entire body you are no longer able to translate because in that process, something will be filtered and therefore lost.

When I watched *Lemonade* for the first time I happened to be with my mother, who had assumed that, because of the ominous trailer, Beyoncé was up to some scary business and therefore initially had no interest in joining me. But she was intrigued by my unblinking eyes, so she sat up and readjusted her head scarf. She asked me to unplug my earphones from my phone so she could listen. In a matter of minutes, she was able to help me formulate an argument with a kind of clarity that made me wonder if she had watched it before the rest of the world. The truth is my mother had been cheated on and betrayed. Unlike me, my mother could mourn for a relationship, a love that she experienced, a marriage to which she was bound, a man who vowed to unite with her, the good times that transpired, the bad times that had passed but were still engraved in her memory like characters on tombstones.

When I logged on to Twitter after the special was over, I realized that I was not alone in my mourning. That night, the social network became a reservoir which black women filled with emotions that they might or might not have been fully able to articulate, but felt within all the grooves of their souls. Beyoncé awakened something in all of us. Her songs laid claim to something dormant in us all, something that we had consciously or unconsciously been hiding. *Lemonade* was not about uplifting black people in general, but rather black women specifically.

IN OCTOBER 2014, THE FRENCH FILM *GIRLHOOD* (*BANDE DE filles*) was released to much critical acclaim. Set in a poor Parisian suburb, the story centers on Marieme, a sixteen-year-old black girl who is failing academically and desperate for a sense of belonging because her workaholic mother and abusive brother cannot provide her with the comfort and support she needs. She eventually befriends a group of other black girls, and although they swear and steal, they are also a tribe that looks after its members. There are true moments of friendship, when they sing Rihanna songs in hotel rooms and dance outdoors, but they engage in vicious fights with other women in rival gangs and attempt to ingratiate themselves with men not out of romantic desire, but rather out of a desire for respect.

Girlhood is magnificent and fatalistic. It is an exploration of how a black girl can or cannot become dominant in a racist and patriarchal society, one in which a path of continual poverty, lacking any upward trajectory, seems to be already determined for both her and her friends. Frames contrasting silky weaves and natural hair, open doors with men lurking beyond every corner, and safe spaces behind closed doors reinforce the idea that this film is not a simple coming-of-age story. *Girlhood* is different not only because the main characters are black, but also because there isn't much emphasis on these teenagers' psychological and moral growth. They are just trying to survive, pushing back on reality every once in a while through song and dance before returning to their hermetically sealed world, which is completely at odds from the popular perception of Paris that centers on the Eiffel Tower and the Champs-Élysées.

Months after I had watched *Girlhood* and on multiple occasions argued that it had raised the bar for a film about teenaged black girls, I found an interview the director, Céline Sciamma, gave to *Indiewire*. Sciamma said, "I'm making this universal, and I decide that my character, who represents the youth of today for me, can be black . . . It's not about race. It's not about struggling with racism." Unlike Marieme and her friends, Sciamma is a white, middle-class woman. Her inspiration for *Girlhood* came from observing "gangs" of young black girls both in and around Parisian shopping centers and the Métro. I am not sure if Sciamma ever spoke to these young black girls, or whether she is aware that groups of black women are not always gang-affiliated, or engaged in fighting and theft. When she saw them, why did she even feel like she had a right to tell their stories? "I had a strong sense of having lived on the outskirts even if I am a middle-class white girl," she told the *Guardian*. "I didn't feel I was making a film about black women but *with* black women—it's not the same. I'm not saying, 'I'm going to tell you what it's like being black in France today'; I just want to give a face to the French youth I'm looking at."

Sciamma is right in that a film involving black female actors is not the same as a film about black women, but the rest of her reasoning falls short. Marieme and her friends were not black women, but black girls. White people readily conflate black girlhood with womanhood because black females are so sexualized that black girls can never be innocent. She also believes that she can relate to these poor, young black girls because like them, she, too, has lived on the margins, despite her being white and middle-class. To believe that, within her middle-class, white female body, Sciamma understands what it means to live on the outskirts of society grates on my nerves. And why does she assume a responsibility to "give a face to the French youth" when she does not even recognize that her understanding of it is framed through her white gaze? Granted, Sciamma has made films with white female protagonists, such as *Water Lilies* and *Tomboy*, but *Girlhood* cannot be analyzed through the same lens. The most obvious reason is because black female representation on screen is so scarce. It is illegal for the French state to gather data about ethnicity and race, but publications such as the *New York Times* have made estimates, and black Parisians only make up perhaps 4 percent of the French population; as such, they are automatically cast as Other. Yet black French girls already have faces and voices. For Sciamma to assert that she can give "a face" to poor black French girls speaks of appropriation, a kind of control that reinforces her role as a white benefactor, and that of her subjects as helpless beings whose stories are not theirs to tell. By providing "a face" to them, she is implying that they themselves are invisible, unworthy of being named, and unable to be named without her assistance.

GIRLHOOD GOT MANY MEDIA CRITICS ARGUING WHETHER nonblack women should write about black women. My criticism of Sciamma doesn't eradicate my feeling that *Girlhood* is one of the best films I've seen in years. I spent hours with one of my former roommates analyzing what black girlhood, femininity, and the juxtaposition of kinky hair versus weaves meant within the narrative, and if I were to watch it again I would find even more symbols and themes to unpack. Karidja Touré, the lead, was spotted on the street (i.e., "street casting") in order to create "alchemy" and "energy."[12] However, the majority of the actresses have not been cast in a high-profile film since. If someone were to ask me if I thought Sciamma did a good job with the story, I would say no: I think that she did a great job. But I also believe that a black woman, especially one from a poor Parisian suburb, could have done an even better job because she would be able to fully engage in the story without being a spectator. I could say the same about the fourth season of the drama series *Orange Is the New Black*, which focused on racism within the prison system and prison brutality towards black women. I found myself enthralled by the storytelling—and annoyed when I found out that no one in the writers' room was a black woman. Issues that concern black women like me were being exploited for profit and consumption by a white mainstream society.

At the 2015 César Awards, Sciamma was nominated for Best Director, and Karidja Touré was nominated for Most Promising Actress. No black woman has won Best Director in the César Awards' history. (Euzhan Palcy, a black Martinican woman and director, was the first black person to win a César Award, for Best First Feature Film, for *Sugar Cane Alley*, back in 1984.) No black woman has ever won a César Award for Best Actress. The first black woman to be nominated in any acting category was Aïssa Maïga, for her performance in *Bamako*, in 2007. In 2016, Déborah Lukumuena became the first black woman and youngest person to win Best Supporting Actress for her role in *Divines*. I want more black, female-centered stories to be written and directed by black women across the diaspora. Women like Beyoncé, Ava DuVernay, Gina Prince-Bythewood, and Amma Asante are making great strides, yet I want more and more and more. But would a black French female director have had the opportunity to direct *Girlhood*? Could I, or anyone else, be comfortable with the fact that if it weren't for Sciamma, already a respected art house director, *Girlhood* might never have received the acclaim that it deserved? The *OITNB* series came from a white, middle-class woman's memoir. Would a black woman's prison memoir have received the same attention and acclaim? Would it have even been published? Given the reality of the systemic barriers, should I resign myself to the fact that at least these stories are being told, even if by nonblack women?

WHY IS THE FILM TITLED *GIRLHOOD* (THE FRENCH TITLE BEing *Bande de filles*, or "Gang of Girls") and not *Black Girlhood*, or even *Marieme*? The truth of the matter is that *Girlhood* is not a "universal" story, despite Sciamma's efforts to make these black girls' experiences collapse into the lie of universality and color blindness. She does not seem to realize that any premise of universality is only facilitated by her white lens, which always assumes whiteness is at the center of any experience. When she declares, "I'm making this universal," "I decide my character," "I just want to give a face to the French youth I'm looking at," she's forcing herself into a narrative that has nothing to do with her. These statements demonstrate how much she wants to have control over a story that was never hers to begin with. This signals to me, as a viewer and a black woman, that Sciamma did not observe these black girls' bodies; she *confiscated* them in order to reproduce the white fallacy that social progress can only be achieved when racial identities are forgotten altogether.

To divorce race and racism from *Girlhood* is to ignore the immense, often invisible forces that restrict the story and the characters. That black girls can simply be girls—that somehow we can share in the deliciousness of being unraced—is a fantasy. It also ejects black girls from being at the center of the narrative, a position in which they have never been privileged to reside.

I only have to think about this in the context of *Lemonade*—a pure, unadulterated visual experience of black women remaining at the center, codirected by a black woman—to realize I do not want to resign myself. Your eyes could not sift through any of the scenes without seeing a black woman, or several. Beyoncé would not allow that. You had to see. You had to watch. You had to stay. You were "going through" just as she was "going through." That is the reality that we had to witness: a black woman's pyrrhic journey, bloodied and beautiful from start to finish, with no hint of white skin to provide momentary relief.

I wish that, for once, a white director or screenwriter could talk about stories featuring women of color without trying to insert him- or herself into the narrative in order to make it more accessible. I do not want a white artist to have either sympathy or empathy for their characters of color. I do not want a white artist to pity a marginalized character's fortune, as this too easily facilitates a savior complex. I also do not want a white artist to imagine him- or herself in the position of that character, because this puts the white experience at the center of a story, whitewashing it altogether. I am not even sure that such empathy for a character of color is possible.

LEMONADE ASKS, *WHAT IS IT LIKE TO BE A BLACK WOMAN IN America?*, and the answer is one no nonblack director or performer could give. She is the most disrespected, unprotected, and neglected person—as quoted from Malcolm X's 1962 speech in *Lemonade*—and also the most resilient. *Lemonade* is not simply a love story, but rather a multilayered portrait of all that the black woman experiences, all the pain that she endures, divided into eleven chapters: Intuition, Denial, Anger, Apathy, Emptiness, Accountability, Reformation, Forgiveness, Resurrection, Hope, and Redemption. One of Beyoncé's biggest strengths is that she is able to lead, and yet also fall into formation herself. Her voice glides through *Lemonade*'s sumptuous visuals of black women, and is often the backdrop against which other black women can exhibit as many tumultuous emotions as she does. This stylistic choice emphasizes that although Beyoncé is a black woman, her experience is different from that of Lesley McFadden, Michael Brown's mother; of actress Amandla Stenberg; of Leah Chase, the "Queen of Creole Cuisine," all of whom appear in the film. Black women are not one thing. In *Lemonade*, healing is not achieved through the individual but through the plurality of community. Beyoncé is supported by a brigade of black women who assist her as she sorts through all of her feelings. They move through the water, hands linked, facing the setting sun as though they are beginning a ritual. They will uplift her not through words but rather through proximity and touch, ushering in self-love and acceptance.

That all of this empowerment takes place within nature enhances the project. Nature is where black women can give themselves permission to indulge in their emotions, and roam around free from any outside forces that may stifle them. The massive oak trees that appear throughout *Lemonade* echo Sethe's chokecherry tree scar in *Beloved*, which represents the horror of slavery and intergenerational trauma. At the same time, trees also symbolize "the healing and regenerative power of nature and community."[13] In *Lemonade*, the stoic black women sitting on top of the tree branches or standing in front of the oaks are there on purpose. Trees stand not only for eternal life but also, of course, for strength. Like the trees themselves, black women stand together, tall and unmoving. Seen together in the final chapter of *Lemonade*, they show that despite their anger and emptiness, they are still alive. Pain does not ravage the black woman's experience; rather, pain embellishes it, for it is through that pain that she recognizes her own tenacity and is reaffirmed by her community, without which she could not survive.

THIS IDEA UNDERMINING *GIRLHOOD*, THAT SAYING *I FEEL FOR you* to a woman unlike yourself means you somehow share in her experience, is one of the pitfalls that plagues mainstream feminism. It signals to women of color that their stories are only worth telling if a white person can understand them, and therefore that a white person's emotions and responses are of greater importance than the stories themselves. We cannot come together if we do not recognize our differences first. These differences are best articulated when women of color occupy the center of the discourse while white women remain silent, actively listen, and do not try to reinforce supremacy by inserting themselves in the middle of the discussion.

In 2015, the rapper Nicki Minaj was snubbed for an MTV VMA nomination for her "Feeling Myself" video, which also featured Beyoncé. Taylor Swift, then America's reigning pop queen, won a nomination for "Bad Blood." Alluding to her "Anaconda" video, which was released the same year as "Bad Blood," Minaj tweeted: "If your video celebrates women with very slim bodies, you will be nominated for vid of the year." Swift, whom the mainstream always seems to protect, responded by tweeting directly to Minaj: "I've done nothing but love & support you. It's unlike you to pit women against each other. Maybe one of the men took your slot . . . If I win, please come up with me!! You're invited to any stage I'm ever on." Minaj was venting her frustration about being a black female artist in a white media world, yet Swift inserted herself into the conversation by positing *herself* as the victim. Other examples of white artists co-opting stories or spaces that are not their own include Kathryn Stockett's *The Help*, and anything Miley Cyrus did in 2013. Any kind of general feminist statement also defaults to whiteness (see Lily Allen's "Hard Out Here" video or Patricia Arquette's historically inaccurate 2015 Oscars speech: "To every woman . . . we fought for everybody else's equal rights. It's our time to have wage equality once and for all and equal rights for women in the United States of America").

For as long as I've been writing, I have struggled with this idea of universality. I would love for anyone to read my black-female-centered work and find themselves engaged. However, I do not believe that readers need to be able to see themselves in my work in order for that to transpire. I do not need a white reader to appropriate African-American vernacular, emphatic gestures, and certain experiences as she tries to figure out where in the narrative she can locate herself to feel closer to the characters. I do not want sympathy but acknowledgment, the freedom to tell an unapologetic story that is both black and female and for people to interact with my words rather than corrupting them altogether to suit their selfish desire to be at the center. I believe that the Otherness of young black girls in Paris fascinated Sciamma, but oftentimes white people's fascination with black girls and women becomes a hotbed for exploitation. If Sciamma believed her narrative to be universal, then that is because she unconsciously placed herself within the story. How else was she going to be able to fill the gaps in her imagination if not with her white, middle-class experience, which often produces a voyeuristic quality when documenting the lives of people of color?

ONE OF THE FEW BLACK FEMALE CRITICS TO WRITE ABOUT *Girlhood*—and positively at that—for a mainstream American publication was Alexis Okeowo, a staff writer at *The New Yorker*. The other reviews and essays that I discovered were mainly favorable ones written by white (mostly male) critics—Mark Kermode in the *Guardian*, A. O. Scott in the *New York Times*, Ann Hornaday in the *Washington Post*, Ty Burr in the *Boston Globe*, Jesse Hassenger for the *A.V. Club*.

There were also reviews of the film by nonblack women of color for significant, but more alternative, online sites such as Fariha Róisín on *The Hairpin*, Durga Chew-Bose on *Buzz-Feed*, and Anupa Mistry for *Jezebel*. I did wonder if any black female writers had pitched those sites to review the film, but at the same time, I enjoyed these commentaries. Cultural criticism, particularly film reviews, is overwhelmingly white and male. I love seeing women of color getting more work in the industry, and I loved that editors had allowed some of these reviews to have titles such as "Finally, a Film about Black Girls Strengthening Each Other" or "On Brown-Girl Exclusivity and Writing Our Own Narrative." But when a nonblack woman of color writes about black women in a way that conflates them with other minorities, particularly under the umbrella of "brown," this label seems diluting. Anti-blackness is pervasive, even among minorities who are also burdened by historical and present-day oppression. It's true that nonblack women of color cannot inflict violence upon black women to the degree that white women can, and have. Women of color do not have that kind of systematic power, and they also suffer in our dominant white patriarchal society. But just because their power isn't systematic does not mean that it does not stigmatize black women and their experiences. Fanta Sylla, a black French writer, confronted this in regards to the film on her personal blog: "Why was the spectatorship of non-black women of color centered instead of that of black women? . . . It is easier to point the finger at white appropriators like the ones cited above than to call out brown cultural writers . . . because what they do is always wrapped in good intentions, always hidden behind faux-semblants of unity and solidarity."

Initially, I was staunchly against Sylla's argument. She seemed to write as though she personally knew the afore-mentioned writers and believed they had an unhealthy obsession with black art. Not to mention, I do personally know one of them and she always seems quite aware of cultural parasitism. I loved all of the nonblack women of color's work, and I thought it was better to have minority women's voices than none at all. After all, they are oppressed by the same white society as I.

It took me over two years of mental fermentation to fully process what Sylla had to say. The influences of race and gender affect all women of color, but these influences function in multitudinous ways. There are times to speak about solidarity between women of color, and times to eliminate the majority of women of color in order to address the issues of one group in particular, that being black girls and women. It's an evergreen demand and conversation across social media channels about only black women writing about black women, and there have been moments when editors responded. For *Lemonade*, Doreen St. Félix wrote about the special for MTV, Brittany Spanos for *Rolling Stone*, Dr. Melissa Harris-Perry for *Elle*. According to Sylla, "the systematic use of this word ['brown'] is how their subconscious desire to erase blackness expresses itself within their language." What need is there to describe us as "brown" other than the deep-seated fear that if our blackness is not diluted through language then somehow we are too distant from everyone else? For a long time I advocated for women of color to use whichever labels made them feel most comfortable, but this was a tactic to avoid conflict. Like Sylla, I eschew the label "brown." I am black, not literally, but racially and politically. "What does this brown identity mean to a Black woman?" Sylla asks. "Brown is a euphemism . . . It feels more like a trap than an identity to me but, I can see why Black people might find this identity desirable. It temporarily relieves you from the burden of blackness."

Black women's experiences are unique among women of color's experiences. Asian women's experiences are unique among women of color's experiences. The list can go on and on. But when we are specifically talking about black women's experiences, the magnifying glass need not move to any other melanin-rich subject. Black women are special. It is we who were captured and transported by the millions to the New World. It is we who needed a divergent branch of feminism to get our issues acknowledged and scrutinized. I use the term "we" because there is very little psychological disassociation between the past and the present when we talk about slavery. What happened during that period directly affects our present. The sexual exploitation during the transatlantic slave trade and the consequential epigenetics that demonstrates that trauma in our DNA is firmly rooted in black people and black female oppression.

When black women are at the center, they are subjected to critique just like anyone else. This criticism feels and reads more bitterly coming from a nonblack female writer, but even if a writer is a black woman and the subject she's critiquing is popular, she might be met with disdain, too. Even if we are in the room by ourselves and writing for ourselves in order to be critiqued by ourselves, if one black woman has an unpopular opinion, which reinforces that we're not a monolith and there is no universal opinion in our group, how do we simultaneously protect the preciousness of our stories and challenge their creators when necessary?

My own response to *Lemonade* was powerful and positive, but it was not met with universal acclaim within the black community. Arguably more so than any other black star, Beyoncé is a divisive figure. A few days after *Lemonade* was released, bell hooks declared in an essay titled "Moving Beyond Pain" that Beyoncé's "construction of feminism cannot be trusted . . . In the world of fantasy feminism, there are no class, sex, and race hierarchies that break down simplified categories of women and men, no call to challenge and change systems of domination, no emphasis on intersectionality. In such a simplified worldview, women gaining the freedom to be like men can be seen as powerful. But it is a false construction of power." This was not the first time bell hooks had criticized Beyoncé. In 2014, during a New School discussion called "Are You Still a Slave? Liberating the Black Female Body," hooks called Beyoncé a terrorist for appearing on the cover of *Time* magazine in scanty attire. hooks was hardly the only critic. Rapper Azealia Banks believed that *Lemonade* peddled the "heartbroken black female narrative" that was the antithesis of feminism, labeling its theme "stupidity," not strength. Ashleigh Shackelford of *Wear Your Voice Mag* argued that *Lemonade* is not for fat black women or femmes because there were none in the special. At the end of her essay, bell hooks concludes that *Lemonade* does not resolve anything, and that healthy self-love can only emerge if black women resist patriarchal romanticization of domination in relationships and refuse to be victims. Once I finished the last line, I felt like a deflated whoopee cushion. Victim? Victim? Is what I'd just watched for a full hour, a portrait of a victim? *Lemonade* was the first time I had seen Beyoncé in an incredibly vulnerable state, and I know her vulnerability was real because I felt it. She is not a fighter against patriarchal domination, but this does not mean she is a victim. She is a feeling black woman, and I realized simply from the criticism of *Lemonade* that as a black woman, if you are not always fighting for something larger than yourself, then you are somehow the enemy, not performing the "correct" form of black womanhood in contemporary America. We should not have to choose between being black, being a woman, and being human in our own story.

WHEN SLAVERY IS DISCUSSED, ESPECIALLY IN THE CONTEXT OF black female slaves, much of the weight is placed upon what was taken from us: our freedom, our language, our bodies. Women were beaten and also raped, and there is nothing that we could do about it. In grade school, there might be mention of how slaves resisted, either through overt rebellion or more subtle methods such as messing with the master's food, working slowly, or faking illness, but these acts are drowned out by the vast, detailed history of how dehumanized we were.

I first learned that I was the descendant of black people who were enslaved when I was around eight or nine years old. My mother and I were sitting in my room when she told me that our ancestors were white people's property and that they were endlessly beaten regardless of whether they performed their duties. We had been brought over here from Africa and forced to work on plantations. Boom. That was it. The common narrative of slavery, the practice of oral storytelling in black households, revolves around two actions:

the beatings and the rapes. I cannot count how many times I've heard from my family and school teachers about slaves having their bodies torn apart by paddy rollers' dogs, or being stripped and staked to the ground so that they could be beaten within an inch of their lives, or having screws jammed into their skin as torture. When my mother told me about slavery, she said, "The masters raped the black women and that's why you're so light now. It's in our blood." As my eyes gazed over my light skin and then the rich brown skin of my mother and sister, I began to look at myself as a mistake. Although my parents loved each other when they'd conceived me, at the base level, I existed because of a violation that took place hundreds of years ago. I wasn't only a product of love but also rape, and as such, I imagined myself as a mutation, an embodiment of corruption.

I understand why this particular approach to black American history is prevalent. Those rapes, that kind of oppressive violence, have warped society. What better way to make clear to another black female about what racism can do to her on an individual level than by telling her that not even her body is her own? Forget about the macrolevel injustices like the school-to-prison pipeline and job discrimination. The rapes get the point across quicker and cleaner, like a blade slicing through a sheet of paper. The whitewashing of atrocities suffered by black people in this country is a regular pastime. In 2010, the Texas Board of Education approved a revised social studies curriculum, treating slavery as a "side issue" of the Civil War, omitting mention of the Ku Klux Klan and Jim Crow laws.[14] That same year Virginia governor Robert McDonnell declared April Confederate History Month;

within the proclamation, he did not cite slavery, saying that he wanted to focus on issues that were more significant.[15] Many historians believe that most slave narratives about life before emancipation focused on victimization because the abolitionist movement demanded the horrors of slavery be emphasized.[16] If you examine movies about slavery, like *12 Years a Slave*, *Django Unchained*, or *Amistad*, very rarely—if at all—will you see slaves laughing with one another.

IN EARLY 2016, SCHOLASTIC PUBLISHED A CHILDREN'S BOOK titled *A Birthday Cake for George Washington*, a story narrated by Delia, the daughter of George Washington's chef Hercules. The book is accompanied by cartoon-style pictures of slaves laughing and smiling. Of course this led to outrage. Kiera Parrott, reviews director of *School Library Journal*, called the book "highly problematic," for the smiling slaves stood in stark contrast to the "reality of slave life." Besides a Change. org petition, the book received one hundred one-star ratings on Amazon.com. As a result, Scholastic pulled the book from the shelves, less than two weeks after its release. What got lost in the narrative was that the author, Ramin Ganeshram, is Trinidadian and Iranian-American. The illustrator, Vanessa Brantley-Newton, and editor, Andrea Davis Pinkney, are both black women. *A Fine Dessert*, a book on a similar theme, was written and illustrated by two white women back in 2014, and it was not pulled. I can speak from firsthand experience about the overwhelming whiteness of the publishing industry and how that might have allowed such a book like this to be published, but the more I thought about it, the more

I realized how complex the issues of authorship surrounding this book are. We mustn't forget that Phyllis Wheatley, the first published black female poet, wrote an ode to George Washington—a man who declared that all men were created equal, yet began owning slaves at eleven and occupied office while hundreds of enslaved black people cooked his food and worked his fields. If a black woman wrote a poem venerating Washington, or illustrated or edited a book arguing that life as a slave had moments of happiness, does that mean that she is a "race traitor"? A more moderate argument is that since the author, although a woman of color, is not a black woman, the slave narrative was not hers to exploit. But what about the illustrator and editor? Evidently, they saw merit in the project. Perhaps *A Birthday Cake* was misguided and misleading; perhaps it wasn't. But what the book did was raise a question as to what constitutes an accurate and honest depiction of slavery. Should we conclude that slaves never laughed? Is it dishonest to say that they never did?

I'm interested not only in what *A Birthday Cake for George Washington* was, but also what it could have been. To erase the wit and comedy of slaves, their ability to laugh, is almost as serious a crime as erasing the abuses they suffered: both strip them of their humanity. Laughter has always been a remedy for black people. When he was interviewed for the *New York Times* by Philip Galanes, alongside Lupita Nyong'o, comedian and *Daily Show* host Trevor Noah explained that humor is "the reason doctors use laughing gas. It's your body protecting you. You laugh until you cry. People understand that once you step into a comic space, there is complete honesty—without judgment." Even enslaved, Africans maintained elements of their folkloric culture, which uses humor as a conduit for anger or rage. It was its own form of violence against the oppressor.

An entirely new world is revealed when we consider this other side of our ancestors, a side that black children especially need to see. I never thought that slaves could laugh. How could they muster up a giggle, or cackle from the root of their belly, if they were constantly being whipped? When would they find the time to smile after a long day's work and perhaps an even longer evening of entertaining masters and their guests?

Much of black humor is developed around the ridicule of white people. As a response, how do we as black people make white people feel like the Other, the outsiders, or—even better—as nonsensical as their rules enforced upon us? Often, the target of the humor is cruel behavior (racist brutality, white supremacy, and so on), but through humor the power dynamics change. We make fun of white people for not being able to dance as well or as fluidly as we can, for aging more quickly, for not chastising their badass children hard enough, or simply for not understanding us, *period*. If you watch any vintage clips of *Def Comedy Jam* or *ComicView*, you'll see this kind of mockery throughout the entire program.

This imbalance—how many of us are still unable to reflect on slavery in a way that foregrounds its horrors while acknowledging slaves' intelligence and agency in spite of them—intrigues me. Perhaps this is why I am tired with contemporary films and historical photos about slavery. They do not explore the fact that although they were legal property, slaves were also human beings who found creative ways to

subvert power and exercise their humanity even after labor-
ing for hours in the blistering southern heat. I would have
endorsed *A Birthday Cake for George Washington* if it had been
about slaves' propensity for making fun of white people right
underneath their noses, which would involve a different kind
of cake.

THE CAKEWALK WAS A DANCE PERFORMED IN THE LATE NINE-
teenth century at slave get-togethers. You lean or rear back
and kick your feet out left and right or vice versa as you move
forward. When I think of the cakewalk, I think of the innumerable times in middle school my black friends and I would
impersonate white girls' attempts to gyrate like us as they
danced. They always missed the mark. What came naturally
to us did not come naturally to them. They thought about
how they danced; they had no sense of natural feeling and
their movements were mechanical.

For black people, bodily expression is spontaneous and
passionate. It is true that after a long day's work the slaves
would sometimes have to entertain the master and his guests,
mainly so that they'd become too tired to think about rebel-
ling. Even if the master had no guests, slaves would still be
dragged into the household to sing, dance, and play music. If
slaves couldn't get a real instrument, such as a violin, they'd
make do with other materials. White people would watch
them dance, fascinated by the exoticness of it all. These
spectacles were purposeful humiliations. But the cakewalk
evolved as slaves' own form of subversion. While serving at
large and fancy parties in the early 1800s, they would watch

well-to-do white people perform strict and stiff dances, like cotillions and quadrilles, and mimic them, exaggerating the bowing and small skips and hops and adding some high steps and jumps. In diaries kept by white people in the antebellum South, the cakewalk is not depicted as a form of satire. After all, why would a sweet slave mock his benevolent master? To white people's eyes, this imitation seemed like flattery. They were delighted that the slaves were attempting their civilized dances. In fact, they would hold competitions and the winning slaves would receive a cake, hence the name. Yet they were being mocked, right in front of their faces.

The performance of the cakewalk is profound considering that slaves' bodies were so subjugated and yet they still found a way to mock their owners, who watched in awe, unaware of their own humiliation through movement and mimicry. In African-American humor, white incomprehension is the basis for many jokes about white people. They cannot understand us and they never will, because they also cannot understand our language.

AFRICAN-AMERICANISTS AND SCHOLARS OF RACE IN AMERICA are well versed in signifying, which is the art of being able to talk around a subject without hitting on the point. Black people play with literal and figurative meanings without even thinking about it. Dr. Henry Louis Gates expounds upon this concept in his book *The Signifying Monkey: A Theory of African-American Literary Criticism*. Our use of our hands and eyes to enhance our stories only opens up more possible interpretations of our words. The dictionary is insufficient

for us because oftentimes our words undermine strict definition. It depends on one's intonation, the situation, and one's
geographical origin. It's hard for me to think of examples
because this reconfiguration of language is innate. It is not
something that I believe you can wholly teach. One may be
"She ain't cut me no slack," and another, "That music was
bangin'": the former representing a burden, and the latter
refiguring what sounds like a nuisance into a compliment.
In learning standard—i.e., white—English, we are taught to
be as direct as possible. African-American English is created
around the idea that indirectness is more fun. Similar to the
cakewalk, our language had to evolve around and underneath dominant white social norms. It's the inscrutability
of our glances, the click of our tongues, the sucking of our
teeth, and our fragmented sentences that communicate our
emotions and character. This is a part of the black experience
that white people cannot entirely access, and this exclusion
gives us fertile ground to ridicule them—our own form of
power.

What does this mean for black female slaves, whose position was unique compared to that of male slaves? In the
United States, it wasn't until the late nineteenth century,
when female comedians first started performing, that critics
decided wit and humor were incompatible with femininity.
However, historically female humor took place less onstage
and more on the page, because in the theater they were rel-
egated to playing masculine women, idiots, or prostitutes.
Harriet Jacobs's *Incidents in the Life of a Slave Girl* is perhaps
the finest example of satire by a black woman.[17] After Nat
Turner's rebellion broke out, slave owners across the South

were scared about what might happen on their property. They had to retaliate, proactively treating their slaves with increased violence to invoke more fear. Jacobs goes into great detail about how drunk soldiers searched houses, whipped black people "till the blood stood in puddles at their feet"— some receiving five hundred lashes—and tortured still others with a bucking paddle. She then exclaims, "What a spectacle was that for a civilized country! A rabble, staggering under intoxication, assuming to be the administrators of justice!"

The humor Jacobs interweaves throughout her elegant prose demonstrates her awareness of the ridiculous society in which she lived. As a writer, she surveys her circumstances, analyzing them bit by bit, to ultimately reveal a different reality: one in which white people, who pride themselves on civilization and respectability, are the real savages. The biting sarcasm of her words allows her to have the upper hand.

This is what I want to tell my future children: slaves knew what was up. Even if they didn't kill their masters, run away, or burn down plantations, slaves suffered horribly and knew that this suffering was wrong—and they had the ability to mine their trauma and find some kind of power within it by humorously belittling their oppressors, stripping them down to the bone to show their inhumanity. White people, not Africans, were the real savages. Enslaved black women were victims, but that's not all that they were.

IN 2013, BEYONCÉ POSED IN A SWEATSHIRT THAT SAID "CAN I Live?" on the front. I am wondering the same for her, and for me, and for all black women. What is our responsibility now? Who will write us? As a black woman, as a descendant of black people who were enslaved—not simply "slaves"—I want to be reminded of our power in spite of our dehumanization. The dominant slave narrative should not be so far removed from that of the human condition. As a black woman, I want to know that despite the cruelty of the slavery, a black man would still have been willing to bear lashes for a black woman; that through the grit of blood between his teeth and the crack of the whip against his back, she was worth loving. As a black woman, I want to know that black people would have kept the wit and spirit needed to spin satire around white slave owners so well that Aristophanes himself would have applauded them. As a black woman, I want to know that white people can never fully know me, break my humanity down to a science, although they have historically tried. I want to know, I want to know, I want to know. I want to know, but not just know. I want to realize that anger metamorphosing into power, that power channeling into humor, that humor gliding past white consciousness, and that white consciousness never being able to fathom what that humor entails. My idea of a black narrative is one that subverts, flips, and undermines rule until that final product cannot be duplicated by anyone other than one with black hands.

Does this mean that only black women should be allowed to write about black women? I am not sure if I can advocate for such a radical position. I do believe that both white women and other women of color can write about black women, but if they do so at a much higher rate than black women do, that's an issue. And furthermore, if they are not willing to self-interrogate while they write about black women and to dismiss universality, color blindness, or dilution of any kind, then no, those individuals (not the entire racial group, mind you) should not write about black women.

The particular experience of the black woman in modern America needs to be addressed. But there isn't just one; there are many. Millions, to be exact. I can only add one.

9

HOW TO SURVIVE: A MANIFESTO ON PARANOIA AND PEACE

1. When you wake up in the morning, thank God, the Universe, or the ancestors that you have been able to see another day. Before your day begins, understand that you opening your eyes again in this world is a triumph in and of itself. Celebrate yourself before you remove yourself from bed, and know that whatever happened yesterday did not kill you, although it might have tried. Your breath may be uneven and your legs may be on the verge of giving out from under you before your feet touch the floor, but you are here. If you can, stretch your arms out towards the ceiling or stretch your smile from one side of your face to

another because this time is the only time you have to yourself before you step out your front door. This is your safe space for self-adulation. Let the praise of yourself lather all over your skin like ointment to prepare you for the world.

2. Once you stand in front of the mirror, do not touch your hair and face yet. Just look at yourself. What do you see? Do you see your mother's eyes or your father's nose, your grandmother's widow's peak or your grandfather's skin? Do you see the ancestors' blessing upon your brow, how their travailing has brought you into existence? Submerge yourself in your beauty. Do not question. Do not filter. Do not judge. Only experience the essence of yourself like a current. Do not impede it with a dam that is there only to diminish just how beautiful you are. Recognize yourself. You are the only person staring back at yourself. Remember this reflection before you leave it because that is the woman you should endeavor to be mindful of first and foremost before you shame your lineage by comparing yourself to anyone else. When you part your coils or curls, shape your fade, buff out your afro, or run your fingers through your strands, move in the direction that feels the most natural to you. You may work in an environment that tries to tame this part of yourself. That is okay. This moment is even more important for you.

3. As you step into the shower, close your eyes and let the water roll down the nape of your neck to the backs of your legs. Water cleanses. Not only must you wash the

sweat from your body but also the energies of other people with whom you both did and did not inter-act the day before. Because you are both black and woman, people want to transfer their energy to your body in hopes that will help them since the body that you're in relays to them that you are always available. Scrub in and around all of your crevices so that no spot can be left untouched before you step out.

4. Clothes. Are you worried that a little bit of leg will make the aunties light-headed even if the only time you see them is at church or at family gatherings? It won't. They have seen much worse in their days, and they probably have done this themselves. Do you wres-tle with the fear that the hint of your breast will have spectators brand you with "whore"? Wrestle no more; they already do. No matter which article of cloth-ing you place over your body, you will have someone think of you as a slut. There is no stitch of fabric that can shield you from them thinking that your body is always available. This is not your fault. It's not because you had sex outside of marriage and everyone knows it. It's not because you let a boy feel you up in middle school when he did not make a commitment to you. It's not because you touch yourself at night. This is an injustice that has been tailor-made for black women like yourself. You just were born into this framework. However, now is not the time to feel defeated before you leave your home. You put on those daisy dukes if you want to. You wear your family earrings or that skirt you feel was not designed with anyone else in

mind but you. For what others think of you is none of your concern.

5. Here comes the hardest part: stepping out your front door. Before walking too far away from your doorknob, close your eyes, breathe in the open air, and let that fill your lungs to their fullest capacity. You're gonna need every particle of it, for there will be people who will want to take your breath away in the most unromantic sense. Now you are on the outside of your home. You are susceptible to any- and everything. At least on the inside, you can turn off the TV, computer, or radio if any content becomes too much. On the outside, you do not have this option, so now you will be able to gauge if your self-adulation in your safe space was either enough or insufficient to prepare you for the story of today. Remember your reflection. Remember the way you touched your hair. Remember the water beads purifying your body. Hold on to that like a boat to an anchor.

6. As you walk to wherever you have to be, do not lower your head to anyone. They are not your God. You are not their children. You still exist in this world, and that should be a source of pride, not shame, for you. Reject that quiver of fear or intimidation you feel toward someone who society esteems more than you. If this quiver is more like an undulation, you will have to work harder to keep it from infiltrating your mind. This is the daily battle that black women have to face, this centuries-old lie that we are less-than when we have been here and will continue to be here before and after

everyone else. If you have not settled with this fact, do it now: you are more than enough. Do you not realize that everyone wants to be you? You have been imitated throughout time and space. You are the arbiter of innovation. When you walk down the street, hold your head high, knowing that what others feign to have, you were organically born with. And they are mad about it because no matter how hard they try, they will never be able to fully consume all that you are. There will always be some part missing, and they recognize this whenever they see you. Regale in this glory.

7. You are not paranoid. When a nonblack person is complimenting you on your eloquence and presentability only because you adhere to the norm, this is not a compliment at all but a salute to white supremacy. You passed *their* test, not your own. We imbue all of our interactions with both implicit and explicit biases. You are being complimented because people do not expect that from you. They don't expect anything from you but a damning statistic. They treat your presence as a cesspool into which they can pour their insecurities because they know their self-doubt cannot be found in your body because the world could not give any less of a damn about you.

8. You are not paranoid. When a nonblack person reaches to touch your hair before asking, they are participating in a centuries-old tradition of conceiving of you as an object, an outlandish thing in the museum of everyday life. You are a spectacle. Dismiss those foreign hands, protecting yourself and your space. You are not

public domain. They want to touch you because they are in awe of you. But do not be fooled: this is not a compliment. This is a learned trait of our environment: to touch what we think will not resist or what we've conditioned to not resist.

9. You are not paranoid. Anytime a person opens the door for him- or herself and closes it when you were right behind them. Anytime a person attempts to cut you in line. Anytime a person interrupts you. Anytime a waiter services white people who have arrived at an establishment many minutes after you. Anytime a person questions what are you doing in a particular neighborhood. Anytime a salesperson does not greet or assist you in a store. Anytime you feel passed up for a promotion. Anytime a person questions your credentials.

10. You are not paranoid. Anytime a person "mistakenly" sits on you on the train or bus. Anytime a little white child points at you. Anytime someone's eyes linger enough for you to be uncomfortable. Anytime a woman tightly holds on to her purse when you sit next to her. Anytime a person changes seats from the one next to you. Anytime you talk and the other person refuses to make eye contact. Anytime someone refuses to shake your hand. Anytime someone tells you to calm down. Anytime someone asks you why you're so angry. Anytime someone asks you why you are so emotional. Anytime someone believes you're thinking too hard or overanalyzing.

11. You are not paranoid. When another black person's body drops to the ground before the earth was ready

to take him back and you mourn as if he or she were your sibling. When another black person's body drops to the ground and you constantly check over your shoulder to see if you will be next. When another black person's body drops to the ground and you fear for the children you have or the children you have yet to conceive. When another black person's body drops to the ground and the rage welling in your spirit stifles your ability to articulate much if anything at all.

12. You are not paranoid. When you need to be silent. When you do not want to talk to anyone out of fear that they will take something away from you that you had yet to identify. When you do not want to be around anyone. When you want to be private. When you protect everything that concerns you, from your mind to your tangible possessions. When your eyes ricochet off the four corners of a given space. When the hairs on the back of your neck and arms stand erect when you enter a place or are around a certain individual.

13. You are not alone. Whenever you dance with a black woman and the two of you are on beat without any instruction, this is not coincidence. This is solidarity. The rhythm of your bodies is rooted in your shared experience, one in which words are useless and the performance is magic to the untrained eye. You do not need to explain. You do not need to rationalize. You just do. And together, you became one in perfect synchronicity with time and space.

14. You are not alone. When you need a moment or several to be in your feelings. When you need to cry.

When you are angry at how you have been mistreated. When all you wanted was a thank-you. When all you wanted was someone who cared. There is another who is experiencing this same kind of lack. There is another who is thinking of you even if you do not know who she is and she does not know who you are. There is a cosmic wavelength of our universal spirit. You do not question. You feel whatever it is that you need to feel and remember that someone is rooting for you. You must believe in this with all of your might.

15. You are not alone. When you are celebrating your successes, however big or small. You are the pride of us all. You are what the ancestors have prayed for.

16. You do not owe anyone anything. No matter how much someone begs and pleads for you to help. No matter who calls on you at the midnight hour to cast their troubles on you. No matter how urgent the request may seem. You do not owe anyone anything. Pay attention when you are tired and have nothing to give, not even your ears. Lie down and rest. The world will be waiting for you when you get back.

17. You are not a mule, despite what others may implicitly tell you. Your back should not be used as a cart within which everyone else stows away their bad news and miscellaneous burdens. That is not your job. You are not to work from sunup until sundown. If you need to seclude yourself, then do so. If the people around you are worth it, they will be there for you when you get back.

18. The revolution is ongoing. It always has been and it

needs you. But you will be unprepared for the task if you run yourself ragged. Do not shame yourself by thinking that you have to fight constantly with little to no rest. You are not an engine. You still have a body to take care of. Do not worry. The revolution will be there when you return.

19. Pay attention to what you take into your eyes and ears, for if you are not careful, you will start to believe that you are going to die sooner rather than later, that Death is at your door, beating away at its surface with a mallet until it has you by the neck. Balance with whimsical and silly content to remind you that the world can be and is a beautiful place in spite of all the grotesquerie.

20. Blackness is an ongoing experience. You may have known that you were a black woman since before your mind could process identities and labels. You may have always known through your family. You may have learned the hard way through the outside world. Either way, you are arriving. There is no singular person who is the authority of your black womanhood. Your experience enriches what we perceive to be blackness and adds another thread to this incomprehensible tapestry. You are irresolute, as we all are, stretching and evolving towards somewhere. Forget about how much time elapsed before you arrived at the start of the journey that had already been transpiring before you could name it. You're here now.

21. There is no one way to be black. Blackness is not a monolith and you are not someone who is lost in the abyss of uniformity. Blackness is a kaleidoscope where, if you look closely, you will see many colorful patterns within the many reflections in the mirror. There is no one way to be black.

22. You are not better than another black person by virtue of your speech, dress, or education. If someone will hate you because you are black, they will do so regardless of your presentation. In fact, that may make them hate you more for trying to become like them. If you believe that you are better than another black person, then you must scrutinize the standard at which you hold them and yourself to see if you are reinforcing white supremacy.

23. You are not just "pretty for a black girl." You are pretty, period. When people qualify your beauty, their mindset has been shattered while looking at your face, and the only way for them to make sense of who they have beheld is to weaken your magnificence. Do not fall for it. Whether or not you realize this, when they leave you, they will be forever changed. That imprint of your face will stay on their minds and leave them in a state of prolonged amazement.

24. You are going to be loved beyond measure. You must believe that with every part of your being. There will be someone who will not demand for you to diminish your black womanhood so that they can feel more comfortable, someone who will not believe that your accomplishments reflect their insufficiency, someone who will listen and allow for you to feel the gamut of emotion.

25. If you stumble across someone who makes you feel guilty for any of the aforementioned traits, make the decision not to love and commit to them any longer than you have. If they apologize, hopefully they will work towards unlearning. Nevertheless, this is not your concern. You do not have to take up the full responsibility of being someone's educator. Yes, there is much to learn, but some have to learn by themselves.

26. When you make love, nakedness does not begin after your clothes are strewn across the floor. Nakedness begins when you strip every shameful memory about your body before penetration. You are not a fast-tailed girl because you crave to connect with someone else. You are not a slut for having been cursed for living in a black female body. Do you know that culture begins in your body? Do you know that when someone enters you, they are pushing into the ancient? When you come, that is rivers and lakes that stream from your body. When someone feasts upon you, that is strength and energy that no apothecary can provide. There are savannahs around your arms and legs, mountains and hills for your breasts and stomach, a delta, roots from the hair that grows to the stretch marks designed on your thighs. You are the start of civilization, and love-making is the pledge of allegiance to all that you are.

27. Forgive your mothers and grandmothers. To what extent is your decision alone. If you do not forgive them, that is your choice as well. But always remember that you are battling to live as they are, fighting between being strong and human, assertive and docile.

28. If or when your body grows with the expectation of a child, there may be temptation to obsess over the baby's looks, especially if the child is a girl. You may worry about her eventual skin color and hair texture. This worry may be exacerbated by other black women who rub your stomach and speculate, too. These are legitimate concerns, for we are still living in this world with all of its stagnant racial and social hierarchies. But do not let these concerns stamp out the excitement that you are bringing life into this world, a life that will be just fine if you affirm her excellence as much as you can. That affirmation begins in the home, that safe space where self-adulation is the arsenal before stepping back out into the world.

29. When you return home after a long day, check in with yourself. How are you feeling? What have you learned? What are you grateful for? What is something that you need to affirm? You can answer these aloud, write them down in your diary, meditate, confess them in prayer. You need this time. Do it as soon as possible so that your emotions will not metastasize into something larger than the contexts in which they were found, wreaking havoc upon your mind and body.

30. When you lie down in bed, turn your face towards the window to allow for the moon to kiss you on the forehead with its light. Close your eyes and take a deep breath in. Allow for your chest to expand as much as it can before you exhale. Whatever happened during the day is done. But you are still here and should revel in that, for this is how you survive.

10

A BLACK GIRL LIKE ME

THERE WAS ONE BLACK FEMALE WRITER WHO I ADMIRED MORE than most others. She was a gorgeous and well-liked person who regularly wrote for the *Guardian* as well as other notable publications. One day, I found out that she admired me, too, for she included me in a list of black female writers whose work she enjoyed. I was elated. Weeks later, I summoned the courage to ask her if she could perhaps talk to one of the editors at the *Guardian* to convince her that I'd be a good person from whom to commission work or to at least give me some advice. She told me she would talk to one of the editors and get back to me. The next day, I received an email from that editor, asking me if I would like to write a quick op-ed. The piece marked the first of many strides, and I thanked my black female colleague for helping me. But she admitted that she hadn't spoken to the editor before that editor reached out to me. *Maybe she didn't get around to it.* I didn't press the issue then. Either way, at least she wanted to help me, I thought.

I yearned to be in New York with the bulk of media and literary people. Despite the fact that I was getting steady work, I still felt like that was not enough. Since I was stuck in New Jersey, I assumed that I was not as respected or visible as my contemporaries because I did not have a 212 or 718 area code. Many days were spent driving forty-five minutes to the nearest Bolt Bus station, another two and a half hours to midtown Manhattan, then another twenty to thirty minutes to interviews for staff writing and editorial assistant positions that would last no longer than fifteen minutes. I knew that I didn't get the job because of radio silence on the employers' end, despite many promising me that I would at least get an email. It was the most psychologically and financially draining time of my life. I couldn't understand why, despite my growing portfolio and Ivy League background, I could hardly get jobs in New York that required an undergraduate degree. But I was still expanding. I found my literary agent, took a coediting job at an indie lit magazine, and wrote widely.

In the months leading up to my move to New York, I was beginning to be followed on Twitter by a Who's Who of New York media, and it felt damn good. People were noticing me, those who I had only dreamed would less than a year earlier, and now I felt like I was moving closer and closer to the elusive "popular table" in this behemoth of a city. But I didn't have many friends in these circles, especially not black women. I hoped that those whom I connected with online would reach out to me once I moved (and I made it known through multiple tweets that I had arrived), but nothing really stuck. Each time I saw photos of brunches with black female writers or long chains that I was not included on that discussed the day's topics, I felt like I had missed my chance. I was too afraid to ask if I could join their hangouts since they were more powerful and successful than I was. Why didn't they reach out? Nevertheless, I made friends and gained mentors, those significantly older than me and people of color, but the vast majority of them were nonblack. I figured that I should give myself time and that many of these people must have known one another for years. I needed to work my way up to become friends with people who held so much clout. It wasn't so much that I wanted contacts but rather a unit of black women who worked in the same industry where we could express our frustration about its blinding whiteness, share our successes, and, of course, help one another through listening or networking.

One day, however, I summoned up the courage to ask another black female writer for a contact at *The New Yorker.* I don't know where I found the confidence to go for such an elite publication, but my mind was turning into somewhat of a boiling pot and I was bubbling over. I needed to move over to larger pots, and my drivenness was igniting the fire that pushed me to go for places within which I had rarely heard of those my age or complexion published. This black female writer was someone who was in the circles that I could only bounce around but never infiltrate. This woman had commissioned an essay from me before, even writing me an extremely adulatory email that I have retained to this day, so I assumed that since she knew my work and her spheres were vast, maybe she could help me get more work. But when I asked her for a contact, she told me that it is better if they—meaning the editors—reach out to me, and I was gobsmacked. Why would *The New Yorker*, of all places, come after me when they could get literally anyone they wanted to grace their publication? I was a twenty-three-year-old writer without a staff position or a book deal. Yes, I was growing in my career, but what the hell would they want with me? How else could there be a space for me there if it were *not* through some kind of pushing? I believed this pushing could best be done with help, and especially from a black woman at that. I expected this because I had been helped many times before.

AT PRINCETON, I WANTED A SPACE TO CALL MY OWN. I HAD access to every book I wanted, every professor; my mental appetite was always sated. Socially, however, I was struggling, and even this is an understatement. I expended much emotional and psychological labor getting dressed up for parties at eating clubs, another campus bastion of exclusivity, and obsessively looked over my shoulder to see if any guy was watching me. I hoped that any guy who talked to me for more than three minutes was interested in me more as a potential girlfriend and less as a potential study partner. And when neither of these aspirations manifested, at least, I thought, I had my writing. In my narrow room, I spent hours creating worlds over which I had more control and power. But soon, wanting to be superior got the best of me and I sought to transport my writing to bigger platforms.

Princeton's Creative Writing Program included big names

such as Paul Muldoon, Chang-rae Lee, Jeffrey Eugenides, Tracy K. Smith, Colson Whitehead, Joyce Carol Oates, and Toni Morrison. Initially, I wasn't interested in the program because I was very protective of my work and prized self-taught refinement over anything else. But after attending an orientation event with my freshman roommate, Ayesha, a Pakistani woman who would become one of my dearest friends, I thought, *Why not?* Ayesha and I had already established a rapport with each other over our love of literature, our closeness to our mothers, and our inability to find boyfriends. It seemed as if we were destined to partake in this new adventure together. So, I ended up applying for an introductory fiction class and she did as well. When the day came for us to check our emails about our candidate status for the program, I watched Ayesha go first. I kept my distance away from her desk so that she could retain a little bit of privacy while reading the email, but judging by her face, I knew exactly what happened. We had exchanged writing samples with each other weeks before we moved into our dorm and I knew how talented she was. She had found a place where she not only was going to fit, but was also destined to excel. When I opened up my in-box and clicked on the email from the Creative Writing Program, I was rejected outright.

Tears spiraled from my eyes before I could gather myself and cry someplace else, away from Ayesha. Being the warmhearted young woman that she was, Ayesha quickly placed a hand on my back and encouraged me to feel that this was not demonstrative of my lack of talent. But being in an institution where status and prestige meant so much, I felt that it was a clear sign that I should give up writing. The following fall, I applied again with an entirely new writing sample and I was outright rejected once more. That was when I realized that enough was enough, and that I would have to lay my Creative Writing Program dreams to the side. Most of the students in the creative writing classes were white, as were those who comprised the most acclaimed and financially strong theater organizations on campus. Basically, I felt like I was out of my league. But I knew I had a voice.

In the beginning, I was an online news writer for the *Daily Princetonian*, but I was hanging on by a thread, both socially and in terms of importance. My assignments were very quick one-off pieces that barely anyone read, and I chose not to attend many of the staff parties because they were nothing but heavy drinking and award giving, but to whom and for what, it was too loud to hear among all the bros. One day, one of the editors asked me if I would be interested in applying to become an opinion writer. I had nothing to lose and all to gain. If I couldn't get into the Creative Writing Program, then surely I could make myself known elsewhere. This time around, I thought I was successful in two ways: one for making the cut and two for being the only black person on staff. I could be special there. I didn't have much time to celebrate because I had to turn around an original piece in a matter of days. My subject? Why the Creative Writing Program was too restrictive. Since it was my first article, I didn't think anyone would pay attention to it. It didn't matter. As long as I saw my name in print, I would at least feel validated that I could keep going with writing. The morning that the article went live, I checked it out on my cell phone and scrolled immediately to the comments section. The first anonymous comment was something like this: "She gets into Princeton because of Affirmative Action and then cries because she's not good enough. It's people like you who should've been rejected. The university doesn't need any more whiny black girls." At first, I was too shocked to be offended. How did the commenter know that I was a woman? My name is unisex. How did the commenter know that I was black? My picture was nowhere in the article. That was when I realized that I was being watched from some imperceptible spot.

Thanks to Facebook and to the many black women whom I considered friends and mentors, word quickly spread throughout the Princeton black community of the vitriolic remarks, and many left comments on my article under their real names in support of what I wrote. There were some, including black graduate students, who emailed the moderator to question why the original anonymous comment was still left up hours after it had been flagged so many times. The outrage led to a forum attended by many Princeton black students. To this day, it warms my heart to think of how many of them, even those with whom I had only shared a few words, were in support of my work. This forum led to the *Daily Princetonian* board releasing a full-length article explaining that anonymous comments need to exist because of free speech, so on and so forth. I wasn't upset because I expected that I would not be protected and I didn't want to be. What no one realized was that when I read that comment, shortly after I processed the gravity of such a remark, I grinned. I don't know if this strength came entirely from myself or because the black women who catalyzed us all gave me what I needed to stand tall.

I PORED OVER *THE NEW YORKER* INTERACTION FOR WEEKS, trying to assess whether I was overreacting. Would I have given a contact to another young black female writer whose work I had commissioned? Yes. Would I have given a contact to another young black female writer who had many bylines to her name? Yes. Why? Because she deserved it. Nepotism has been reserved for the white and wealthy for too long. Given that mainstream media feeds off black people and their ideas yet hires them at disproportionately lower rates, I do not consider this kind of assistance mere generosity and amiability but a cultural duty for those like me. It would be cruel for me to climb up a ladder and pull that ladder up as I go. This black female writer I had contacted already had enormous influence and a career that many toiled to have. I thought that if she didn't feel comfortable sharing contacts, then she could have let me know and I would have understood. But then again, what would it benefit her to withhold contacts from me?

The act of withholding is a part of the crabs-in-a-barrel theory that stymies black people in general and, in this case, black women specifically. Our race and gender disenfranchises us; our art often leads to swift rebuke, even from other black people. History has shown us this before: both Alain Locke and Richard Wright blasted Zora Neale Hurston's *Their Eyes Were Watching God*, calling it "oversimplification" and exploitation of "Negro life" for white audiences, respectively. How do we hold on to our individuality and freedom of expression if we are always held to account to the overarching, ever-elusive black community? There is this constant desire to take for ourselves because only a few of us are ever going to succeed. We have been taught that anyone who tries to grab on to our coattails needs to be pushed back down into the abyss where they belong. I've heard of this crabs-in-a-barrel concept since I was a child, and it's so pervasive that I don't know where or by whom exactly I was first informed of its poison. Never did I or anyone else in my community take into consideration that some crabs are at higher positions than others. Is it their fault that the lower crabs want to climb and see the light by any means necessary? Why haven't we taken into consideration that all of us are warring within a contained space before someone outside of our group decides to lift the lid of that barrel?

Perhaps there cannot be too many of us because then we won't be special anymore. It feels good to be special because you're seen as the beacon set upon a hill, a lighthouse illuminating the dark sea. Everyone else within that sea knows and sees you, but you don't necessarily have to see them. Until you finally wake up and realize that it was all an illusion. You are not special; you are tokenized, thrust out into the open to perpetuate the lie that America is the land of equal opportunity. You are expected to be yourself, but not so much that you forget which spaces you occupy, those in which you are the only one or one of very few. You are outnumbered, and you can either fight to change the game or be so broken by playing the game that you fall in line. At least the latter promises that you'll be safe, although by how much and how long, no one else is to say.

Black women, especially those who are writers, exist in a continuum of attacks on all sides. It is natural to want to focus on individual survival because no one else will look out for us. Mainstream feminism won't. Nonblack women won't. Black men won't. White men certainly won't. We are both precious and precarious. But if we don't value and support our individual, disparate experiences, who will?

When aspiring black female writers email me to ask questions, I respond promptly. When I am asked for contacts, I give them. I do not want to leave this earth knowing that I had a sumptuous feast while other black women had a pittance. But I am not immune to tokenism and crab survival. I do wonder if I'm being too nice to complete strangers, those whose works I haven't commissioned, and they need to struggle a little bit more. Be more proactive in their approach. My heart used to palpitate whenever I saw another black girl get published somewhere great, even if I'd written for that publication months prior. I grew anxious if I wasn't included in lists of black writers to follow on Twitter or link roundups of pieces by black women—it was as if when the other black girl had her shine, somehow that robbed me of mine.

One of the greatest mistakes for black women is believing that solidarity ruins their individual trajectories and that in order to protect themselves, they must repel those most like them in shared oppression. I do not agree that every black woman has to be friends with every other black woman whom she meets. We all have different value systems that will logically make us incompatible to some or many. However, we must criticize when those who have become more successful and white-adjacent than others have not made an effort to lift another up in order to dilute that blinding whiteness. We have the responsibility to bring other black women to the forefront of the culture we've helped to create and sustain.

I THINK BACK TO WHEN I WAS TEN YEARS OLD, A LITTLE BLACK girl who thought that making an all-white cheerleading squad would make her more acceptable and beautiful. I think of that ten-year-old black girl who was sycophantic to the white girls trying out in hopes that she would be liked. I think of that ten-year-old black girl who manipulated her smile and body to appease the all-white judging panel for a spot on the team. I think of that same ten-year-old black girl whose white so-called friends got in, barely looking her in the face once they passed through those doors to celebrate with the rest of their squad. And I think of who I was at Princeton: a nineteen-year-old black woman who angered some anonymous person by being in an elite space. I had to be reminded of my blackness and womanhood because those two identity markers were supposedly the things that put me in a bind.

Back then, I wasn't opinionated; I was whiny. I wasn't smart; I was foolish. I wasn't accepted; I was taken in out of pity. I grinned. I grinned and I grinned and I grinned some more. What the experience taught me was that I had, in a sense, made it to a place where I was never supposed to be. Someone tried to put me in my place, but it was too late. I was already all up in the space, reading the same books, taking the same classes, studying with the same professors, and eating alongside them at the same dining halls. For every hint of brown that they saw, their minds went haywire. Every black girl present caused a disruption. It was not only our presence that made them mad, but our excellence. They might have had the privilege not to conceptualize black women in their spaces, but now they saw them in the flesh, moving and navigating just like them. This was their nightmare and my joy.

Surprise.

You should've known I was coming.

ACKNOWLEDGMENTS

Dear Mom and Dad, I know some parts of this book may have made you gasp or clutch your chest but I love you dearly and I am blessed to be called your daughter. Thank you for believing in me even though I cast that former dream of being a doctor aside. Everything I write is in honor of you.

To my four beautiful sisters and my eight nieces and nephews, I love you all. No matter how much we get wrapped in our own respective lives, I can still feel your love and support no matter where I am. I hope you can feel mine as well. To the rest of my family—stepmother, uncles, brothers-in-law, aunts, nieces, nephews, grandparents, cousins—I love you.

To my late stepfather, I hope you're entertaining all the angels up there with your stories. I also hope you're proud of me.

I would like to thank Monica Odom, my wonderful literary agent, who took a chance on a small-town New Jerseyan writer when no one else would.

To the Harper Perennial team—Sofia Groopman, Amy Baker, Danny Vasquez, Megan Looney, Mary Sasso, Amanda Pelletier, Kim Racon, Tina Andreadis—thank you for your immense support and the ability to respond to emails very, very quickly.

Hannah Wood, thank you for acquiring this book. I never would've imagined that a chance dinner over Ethiopian food in Harlem would lead us to be a part of each other's lives in this way. I am indebted to you.

Thank you to Alex Chee, Porochista Khakpour, Ashley Ford, and Alana Massey for being my early readers and for bestowing upon me compliments that I will carry with me for as long as I keep writing.

Thank you to Jade, Dion, Liz, Maraiya, Safy, Suleika, Aric, Angela, Alli, Stephanie, Brandon, Sarah, and Suzan for reminding me that although writing is what I do, that's not all that I am. If I missed your name and you've known me for a while, my apologies. This is a lot of pressure to remember all at once! Your laughs and your open ears and hearts have carried me tremendously throughout this journey.

Thank you to Princeton and the Bennington MFA program for shaping this once insecure girl into a fearless woman who questions and listens but also resists and challenges when necessary.

Thank you to Catapult, particularly Andy, Yuka, and Mensah, for pushing my writing to another stratosphere of artistry.

Thank you to you, reader, for trusting me enough along this journey full of my darkest moments and most triumphant strides. We made it together.

Thank you, God, for never leaving me when I was too afraid to write my honesty, giving me peace that surpasses understanding when an assignment is complete, and endowing me with grace to pick up and start again the next day.

NOTES

3. THE STRANGER AT THE CARNIVAL

1. It's important to note that a black girl's perm is not the same as a white girl's. In the black community, a perm and a chemical relaxer are synonymous. The end goal is to make the hair straight, not curly.

2. Dr. Melanye Maclin-Carroll recounted this in Chris Rock's 2009 documentary, *Good Hair.*

3. Read Tabora A. Johnson and Teiahsha Bankhead's "Hair It Is: Examining the Experiences of Black Women with Natural Hair" and Victoria Sherrow's *Encyclopedia of Hair: A Cultural History.*

4. Dress codes for girls are generally more restrictive, anyway. According to the Women's Media Center, in one two-week period in 2014, two hundred students from Tottenville High School in Staten Island were cited for dress code violations. Ninety percent were girls. This is how slut-shaming starts. In 2015, Macy Edgerly, a then-honors student and high school senior at Orangefield High School in Orange County, Texas, was sent home for wearing yoga pants and an over-

sized shirt. We teach young girls that they can distract male teachers and students with their appearance, and that it is their responsibility to curate their appearance responsibly to avoid inciting the risqué fantasies of passersby. Members of the American Psychological Association Task Force on the Sexualization of Girls found that self-objectification occurs when girls "learn to think of and treat their own bodies as objects of others' desire." When we shame young women for bare midriffs, spaghetti strap tops, or showing their legs, we are inadvertently teaching them that their bodies are more important than their minds, and that their bodies are inherently objectified and sexualized for just taking up space. Repercussions from these rules include poor school performance, low self-esteem, and eating disorders. For black female students, culturally charged ethnic and natural hairstyles further complicate this intersection of appropriateness and modesty with identity and the body. If a black girl wears her hair in dreadlocks, cornrows, afro-puffs, or twists, how is she being a distraction? Who is she distracting? If she is not "presentable," who decides that?

5. In predominately white films and TV shows, curly, thick hair is often presented as something that needs to be transformed. The character Mia Thermopolis, of *The Princess Diaries*, has her hair cut and flat-ironed to appear more regal before she assumes her position as princess of Genovia. The characters played by Julia Roberts in *Pretty Woman*, Anne Hathaway in *The Devil Wears Prada*, and Sandra Bullock in *Miss Conge-*

niality all straighten their hair to signify a positive aesthetic transformation. In *Clueless*, Tai Frasier's curly reddish hair is pressed with a flat iron as part of her makeup. It's interesting to note that compared to the blonde, straight-haired Cher, Tai is sexually experienced. To become more sexually appealing and daring to Danny, straight-haired goody-two-shoes Sandy, in *Grease*, curls and buffs out her hair. But for black women, sexuality is not so transmutable. Our sexualization is immutable in the bodies that we inhabit.

5. A LOTUS FOR MICHELLE

6. Shailagh Murray, "A Family Tree Rooted in American Soil," *Washington Post*, October 2, 2008, http://www.washingtonpost.com/wp-dyn/content/story/2008/10/01/ST2008100103245.html.

6. BLACK GIRL MAGIC

7. Clover Hope, "Who Gets to Own 'Black Girl Magic'?," *Jezebel*, April 7, 2017, http://jezebel.com/who-gets-to-own-black-girl-magic-1793924053.

8. *Women with Disabilities: Essays in Psychology, Culture, and Politics*, edited by Michelle Fine and Adrienne Asch.

9. http://academic.udayton.edu/race/03justice/crime09.htm.

10. James Henry Hammond, a South Carolinian slave owner, believed that some of his slaves were conjure practitioners who were vandalizing and stealing on his estate. Much to his chagrin, Hammond was unable to

find proof of his suspicion, and his slaves believed that they were supernaturally protected, existing on another metaphysical plane to which Hammond had no access.

11. Yvonne Chireau, *Black Magic: Religion and the African American Conjuring Tradition.*

8. WHO WILL WRITE US?

12. Alison Nastasi, "'Girlhood' Director Céline Sciamma on Reclaiming Childhood, Casting Her Girl Gang, and How Her Film Mirrors 'Boyhood,'" *Flavorwire*, January 30, 2015, http://flavorwire.com/502100/girlhood-director-celine-sciamma-on-reclaiming-childhood-casting-her-girl-gang-and-how-her-film-mirrors-boyhood.

13. William J. Terrill of Monmouth College in his paper "Sacred Groves and the 'Jungle Whitefolks Planted': The Dynamic Symbolism of Trees in *Beloved*."

14. Bobby Finger, "Here's How New Texas Public School Textbooks Write about Slavery," *Jezebel*, September 1, 2015, http://jezebel.com/heres-how-new-texas-public-school-textbooks-write-about-1726786557.

15. "Whitewashing of Slavery Embarrasses Virginia Governor," SPLC *Intelligence Report*, Summer 2010.

16. Meghan Hilbruner, "'It Ain't No Cake Walk': The Influence of African American Music and Dance on the American Cultural Landscape," *Virginia Social Science Journal* 50 (March 2015).

17. Glenda Carpio, *Laughing Fit to Kill: Black Humor in the Fictions of Slavery.*

ABOUT THE AUTHOR

MORGAN JERKINS IS A HARLEM-BASED WRITER AND CONTRIB-uting editor for *Catapult*. She graduated from Princeton University with an AB in comparative literature, specializing in nineteenth-century Russian literature and postwar modern Japanese literature, and she has an MFA from the Bennington Writing Seminars. Her work has been featured in *The New Yorker*, *Vogue*, the *New York Times*, *The Atlantic*, *Elle*, *Rolling Stone*, *The Guardian* (London), and *BuzzFeed*, among many others.